(Have Yourself a)

Happy Hygge

Christmas

by

Jo Kneale.

How to have a happier Holiday Season using the Danish principle of hygge to keep it silent, calm and bright.

Contents

The Celebrations of Winter: Thanksgiving, Hanukkah, Diwali and Winter Solstice. 67

Christmas Hygge with your Wide Circle of Family and Friends 86

Copyright

Dedication:

This book is dedicated

with much love

to my Brothers;

Without whom the Christmases of my childhood

wouldn't have been the same.

As Donkey says in **Shrek The Halls**,

"Christmas isn't Christmas until somebody cries,

and usually that someone's me."

About the Author

Jo Kneale has been a teacher, a mother, a teacher again, a teaching assistant and now an Office Ninja for her husband's law firm, Peter Kneale Solicitor. She's been good at hygge since she can remember, but only had a word for it in the last five years, when an unhealthy obsession with The Killing led to a fascination with all things Danish, Scandinavian and a love of the concepts of hygge, lykke and lagom.

Add that to a passion for all things Christmassy, and a book about making Christmas hyggely was inevitable. Christmas is peak hygge season.

Married for nearly 24 years to Peter, she has three teenage children and seven guinea pigs at present. She likes to read, watch Game of Thrones, House and West Wing, visit cities with her husband and make things.

She always wanted to write a book, and writing about hygge is what she does almost daily on her blog, How to Hygge the British Way. Her first book, 50 Ways to Hygge the British Way, was published in March 2017 and her second book, How to Hygge Your Summer, came out in time for her birthday. Both are available from Amazon in Kindle and paperback form.

Jo believes that everybody can enjoy more hygge in their lives, they just have to recognise it, own it and hashtag it. If you're interested in learning more about Jo's style of British Hygge, then visit the website, www.howtohyggethebritishway.com or join The Hygge Nook group on Facebook. And for a beautifully hygge take on Christmas, join The Christmas Party on Facebook.

Introduction

Christmas has got to be one of the most magical, beautiful, lovely, warm times of the year. It is peak hygge season, a time for spending with friends and family.

It's also one of the most expensive, stressful, busy and noisy times of the year.

Those two aren't incompatible, but they do need working at to make them fit together comfortably. Christmas takes effort and, for many people, a crazy amount of money. According to one report, the cost of Christmas in 2016 worked out at £174 per household for the food alone on Christmas Day and £45 per adult just for the booze![1] Christmas takes up any spare cash in December and many will still be paying off the cost of last Christmas when this Christmas rolls around!

Is that inevitable, though? Is there a different way to do Christmas, without debt and bills smothering the Christmas cards as soon as January appears? Can we have a Christmas with time to chill, time to enjoy family and friends, time to relax over the mince pies and still enjoy a turkey and all the trimmings?

---

[1]   http://www.independent.co.uk/money/the-real-cost-of-christmas-a7474156.html

Is a busy Christmas full of stress inevitable?

Well, yes and no.

Christmas will always carry a degree of stress, simply because we're trying to produce magic without being magicians. We want the Christmas Cake and to eat it, we want to produce the snow, the cards, the whole TV ad-perfect Christmas without it taking too much time and money... the two things it invariably always needs.

If you want the all-singing, all-dancing advert-perfect Christmas and you want to have a peaceful season free from debt as well, then you're probably not going to be happy by the end of the month. There are too many demands on our time and cash for them all to be fulfilled. You will either have to accept that, or die trying.

But you can have a Happy Christmas, a season of love and peace and joy if you're prepared to re-think it. To realign your holiday celebrations with your deepest needs, and to let go of some of society's expectations and your own. More specifically, you can have a very happy Christmas if you work hard to make it hyggely.

What do we mean by Hyggely?

Hygge is the Danish idea of contented, safe, comforting, cosy, happy time spent alone or with friends. It's the word Danes use about almost anything... a comfortable café can be hygge, a walk in the woods can be hyggely, a night playing boards games or sipping mulled wine can be hyggely. These events are not hyggely in and of themselves, but the feelings surrounding them make the hygge.

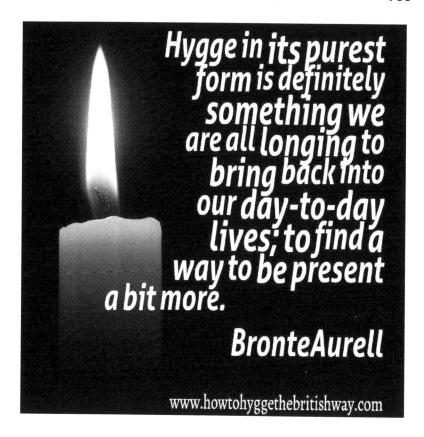

Hygge in its purest form is definitely something we are all longing to bring back into our day-to-day lives; to find a way to be present a bit more.

BronteAurell

www.howtohyggethebritishway.com

Hygge is a way of noticing and being grateful for the special moments in your life, a way of finding pleasure and solace and happiness in small things. It's not mindfulness, it lacks enough pretention to be the same as mindfulness, but it does ask for engagement and involvement in the simple pleasures of life.

As I wrote in my book, How to Hygge Your Summer[2], "hygge is a way of looking at and feeling about life. It's an appreciation of the lovely things in life, both human and inanimate. It's about appreciating what we have and sharing that with others. It's about creating a safe space where people can get together and be confident that they won't be criticised, won't feel isolated, won't be afraid to share their thoughts and feelings as long as they are prepared to accept everybody else in the same spirit."

Creating safe spaces to get together and share? Appreciating what we have and sharing that with others? Gathering people to prevent isolation? Isn't that Christmas entertaining in a nutshell?

Of course, there are conditions to creating that safe space. There's making sure nobody feels awkward because of another person's views that are being too freely expressed. There's making sure that you aren't doing this just to impress or to show off, but truly to enjoy the season and the company, and there's making sure that your guests or your hosts enjoy the experience as well.

Hygge works best in a place where the people agree, for the sake of unity, to set aside any differences in race, religion, politics or football

---

[2]https://www.amazon.co.uk/How-Hygge-Your-Summer-Hyggely-ebook/dp/B071HYD7SL/ref=sr_1_2?ie=UTF8&qid=1501232119&sr=8-2&keywords=how+to+hygge

and agree (even if only by tacit consent rather than a mass discussion) not to mention anything that might cause ill-feeling. We could all tell stories about an intolerant relative, young or old, who just doesn't get why it might be better not to hammer on about their pet peeve at this precise moment, as the rest of the gathering watch a different relative turn purple because they hold completely opposite views but don't want to cause World War Three over the pudding.

May you have warmth in your igloo, oil in your lamp, and peace in your heart.

Eskimo Proverb

www.howtohyggethebritishway.com

How much better to have talked through the possible conflicts with both sides before. Setting up a cease-fire and asking them to hold their views private for one day isn't unreasonable, especially since Christmas, the day of peace, should be a time when we can meet and set those differences aside. If they can agree to honour their common humanity at that point in time and space, and to focus on the things that keep us bound together as humans, rather than the things that separate us as tribes, then Christmas is the perfect time to try to live by these tenets.

So how do we go about making Christmas into a haven of hygge?

Well, we need to look at the different ways we celebrate the season of goodwill and to think how we can bring the concept of hygge to bear in each one. We need to take time in advance of the Christmas season, which for most people now lasts the whole of December, and plan ahead for events, gatherings and meetings that will not leave us frazzled, but allow us the grace to get to the end of Christmas (and, like Charles Dickens, I count that as Twelfth Night and the removal of all the Christmas fripperies) with a smile on our face at least, if not the heart-warming feeling that somebody, somewhere has been left better off by the fact that we celebrated.

Christmas, Chanukah, Solstice…. The Celebrations go on and on…

At this time of year, there are reasons to celebrate every few weeks from the end of October until mid-January. In this book I'm not very confident at dealing with feasts I know very little about. I'm not an American, so I can't speak about Thanksgiving. I'm not Jewish, so the intricacies of Hanukkah are beyond me, I don't know enough about the solar year to talk about Solstice celebrations with great confidence. I have included mention of festivals where I'm aware there's a link, or a chance to learn more about another culture, but in doing so I speak from research rather than personal experience myself. I have also relied on the advice and counsel of Hygge Nook members from different religions and nations, who are always really rather good at advice and information when I need it.

Most information about alternative winter festivals is included as part of a separate chapter, although I could have included it in the chapter about our Wide Circle of Family and Friends, on the basis that you probably have links with people who celebrate other feasts in your wider acquaintance.

A Word About the Religious Festival or the Pagan Feast

I am a Christian (baptised Catholic, confirmed Anglican, ordained … well, nothing & not likely to be. I am a most unholy person) and I mostly approach Christmas personally from the point of view of celebrating the birth of Jesus, with the Angels, shepherds, three wise men and all. But I'm also a Mother of Atheists and enough of a history buff to know and admit that perhaps... **just maybe**... Christianity stole the whole Christmastime/Midwinter Festival idea from the Pagans.

It makes sense to me, though. The celebration of the year's turning from darkness into light and the associated relief of worry that that must have brought has been celebrated by mankind since... well, probably since some woman pointed it out to him and made him a cup of something to sip as he watched the Sol Invictus rise triumphant after the Longest Night.

In this book, I recommend several Holy Things to do both inside and out of the home. I know several of you will do these already, and see celebrating faith as perfectly natural and wonderful to do. That's great, and I hope this book will only aid you in that practice.

If you are dead set against faith, there's no pressure. Just ignore that advice and replace it with things that suit you, but I have to put a good word here in for most Churches and faith groups I know: if you want quiet, contemplative and spiritual (small s) atmospheres, then Church (big C) has an advantage there. They have lots of years of experience at doing it. If I suggest a Midnight service, I'm not asking you to convert, just to sit quietly and think your own thoughts in surroundings designed to help you do just that.

Likewise, for a good blood-pounding sing along you can't beat a carol service. Go, join in, don't feel obliged to become a member, or even to ever go back again. That's the great thing about Christmas: the churches I know expect people to visit at Christmas who never come again for the whole length of the year. They won't raise a murmur if you sidle in quietly, enjoy the experience and then vanish like the mist.

I also recommend being charitable at Christmas. The rewards for being a cheerful giver are well-recorded. It does actually make you feel better and I think it builds a sense of gratitude into your life. I have made no specific recommendations for charities. Like hygge, the charities we support are intensely private.

Holy or unholy, Christmas is what you want it to be. It is possible to celebrate both The Light **of** the World and the light **in** the world at the same time, and that's what I'm aiming for. No argument, see? Holy Hygge!

Another Word about Lagom and Lykke

Because the media are always in search of the next Big Thing, there was a lot of talk in the summer of 2017 about Lagom as being the New Hygge. That's not necessary.

Lagom is the old Swedish principle of enough. As in, take enough to be happy and enough so that everyone can have a share. It's about seeking a Goldilocks Lifestyle, not too hot, not too cold, just right. It fits in nicely with hygge, because hygge is never about ostentation, showing off, conspicuous consumption or anything requiring a massive spend on fripperies. It's actually a principle that underlies a truly hygge Christmas: how can we party when others go hungry, and why should we spend so much money for no return are thoughts that both play a part in creating a meaningful, hyggely Christmas.

A large part of this book is asking you to think what is enough for you, and how can you keep your Christmas balanced in time, energy and expenditure. If you've seen the word, and want to know more about living life in balance, can I recommend two books on Lagom (and both called Lagom, actually) by Linnea Dunne and Anna Brones. They'd make excellent Christmas presents for anybody who's searching for more balance in their life.

In this book, I won't talk about Lagom a lot. Partly because this book is consciously concentrating on hygge, partly because I'm hoping to get another book about balanced Christmas out of it (joke), but mostly because lagom, to a large part, is common sense.

Christmas is a tonic for our souls. It moves us to think of others rather than of ourselves. It directs our thoughts to giving.

B. C. Forbes

www.howtohyggethebritishway.com

Over spending, over-eating, over-consumption of resources is never pretty. Have a party, yes.... But then be sensible and rest tomorrow. Or have a walk in nature. You know, keep life balanced. Have a day of excess, or perhaps the week, but balance that with a few days of normal eating and exercise. A whole month of excess is too much for spirit, body and mind to go through. Balance.

And Lykke, which hit the bookshops in September 2017 with the publication of Meik Wiking's second book, The Little Book of Lykke, is just the Danish word for happiness. I could have called this book Lykke Hygge Christmas, but that would just be bragging and using a word because I've learnt it and want to show off. Lykke comes with hygge, because to hygge is to be happy.

How is the book structured?

The book starts by asking you to think through Christmas past, present and future. It asks that you make a few notes and lists, ready to prioritise the things that really mean Christmas to you and your family. I haven't included any empty pages for you to make notes. I'm expecting you either to have a Christmas notebook that you can spare a few pages in, or to create a notebook to make lists, record quotes and generally plan your season in.

Then it starts to draw concentric circles, starting with the widest one, the World, and gradually getting smaller and smaller until we come in the last chapter to you, and how to keep your personal Christmas hyggely. Read the book in order, or skip to the chapter that you need most advice on, whichever works for you. Each chapter has a section marked Action!!! with just a couple of ideas to take away with you. Christmas is complicated and pressured enough without a list of impossible things to achieve in the next 24 hours. I'm happy if you read the book, enjoy it, get a couple of ideas and then go away and do what suits you and your household best.

Then there is the resources section: as many of the films, books, articles and websites I can remember that have helped me to build the Christmas that suits me and my family. I hope they will help you as well.

But first, let's start by thinking: what makes Christmas for you?

What makes for a Happy Christmas for you?

Spend a couple of minutes now just thinking about Christmases in the past. You want to get yourself a notepad and pen, a warm mug of tea (Chai, for a wonderful Christmas scent as you drink) and to settle into a quiet spot where you won't be disturbed.

Go back to your childhood. What are your most immediate memories of that time? Does any particular event stand out? A special visitor? A meal somewhere? Spending Christmas with relatives or friends? It can be useful here to ask the family as well, get the whole house involved. The things that make Christmas for you may not be the same for other people.

Think of the most Christmassy feeling you've ever had: can you imagine every detail? What made it Christmas for you? What emotions do you remember? Which people were there? What were you doing?

Keep working through your Christmas memories and making notes. It may be that a particular cookie you ate one year has made an impact, or the colour of the decorations on a tree in your Aunt's house. It could be that your Christmas memories are all bad ones, and you want to forget them, in which case please do. You need to start from a happier time and build on that, even if today is your happier time. You may need, in that case, to adopt some happier memories from other people. Be like Frank Cross in Scrooged, whose childhood memories all came from the television shows he watched as a child.

You are looking to build up a sensory blanket to surround yourself with, so that this can be the base upon which you build your Christmas wish-list.

My notes would read something like this:

Childhood: The smell of mince pies baking, the laughter watching **Morecambe and Wise** altogether as a family, the sound of music playing on the record player. A K-Tel record with a pop-up Santa's Village inside, the Concert Band we belonged to playing carols in the centre of our town, cold hands playing a clarinet, warm tomato soup in a plastic cup, the scent of cinnamon, a tin of Quality Street to share, dates and figs. The smell of oranges being peeled and eaten. My Nan eating dark chocolate ginger and sharing them with me.

Early Married life: Learning how to bake a turkey, eating the bacon off the top of the turkey after Midnight Mass. Having in-laws on Christmas Day, icing a Christmas Cake. Getting a Christmas music cd every year to be the background music for that year. Having time to make cards for everyone!

Christmas as a Parent: wrapping presents that are just too weird to be wrapped, going to a whole family Christmas because the children wanted to be with their cousins, having aged relatives for Christmas dinner, Family Traditions like looking at the lights in the neighbourhood, watching the same programmes on Christmas Day, reading the Christmas books. Present giving traditions (stockings, in between gifts) and online/offline shopping. The Traditional Visit to Santa.

Christmas now: Less shopping, because teenage children prefer money, Christmas at my house again, still traditional all-around-the-telly programmes, but the night lasts longer because we all stay up for the adult programmes as well. New traditions with daughter and sons. No visits to Santa but family visits to the cinema instead. Celebrating small. No big parties. Days out to the sales or to the woods. Plenty of sweet treats, baking with cinnamon. Events not things. Finding me time somewhere. Candles, oranges, decorations, a new Christmas music cd on download now. **Living the hygge lifestyle**.

Can you see how my Christmas memories have changed throughout the years? That's because life changes. People come into and out of our lives and we need to move on. It's often said that the first Christmas after someone dies is the hardest. I'd argue for the second or third. The first one can be written off almost as a temporary affair, but the fact that they aren't with us the year after is harder, since it makes it a more permanent loss.

And you can see how pretty much all the senses are involved in the celebration of Christmas. Sight, sound, touch, taste and scent all play a part in building memories. When you're thinking through your ideal Christmas you may want to think about which features of your Christmas appeal to which sense.

The list isn't just to look at and smile at, though. Use it to build lists for yourself as the basis of your Christmas going forward. For example, I know that my Christmas works best with a good dose of cinnamon, so I try and build that in using either scented products or, for preference, a hefty amount of baking that I can share with people. Music plays an important part, and has done since childhood. I love finding quirky versions of old favourites, or rediscovering ancient favourites. I'm listening to Bing Crosby singing **Mele Kalikimaka** as I write this, but it could just as well be Pink Martini or Twisted Sister. I will always look out for a new Christmas CD to add to my collection. After a few years, I can remember the Christmas by the music of the year. 1997 was Evita. 2014 was Bob Dylan. 2016 was Kylie.

I also know that my happiest Christmas days have been spent at home, doing the cooking and setting the table. Yes, it's work, but it's work I enjoy for people I love. I am quite philosophical that when the offspring grow up, that will have to change and maybe... just maybe... when I'm older I'll be the one visiting other houses and being cooked for, but for the present the job is mine and I love it.

Finally, I like getting the family to do things together. Whether that's watching a TV show, going to the movies or visiting a city, I'll build that it to my Christmas as well.

I'm hoping your mind is running away at the moment, with a list of things that you want to get done now you've thought of them. Slow down... hold your horses. Sit back, read the rest of the book and make notes as you go along. Every chapter has suggestions for actions, or links to books and websites in, so it would be a shame to plan your Christmas without checking them out. There may be a really good idea awaiting you just around the corner......

Action!!!

- Get your Christmas notebook out and start making a list of the things you remember from your youth.
- Start a Pinterest board on Christmas. It's such a useful place to put the recipes, ideas and inspiration you want to look at. I have my Christmas split into home decoration, recipes and crafts.

Christmas is the day that holds all time together.

Alexander Smith

www.howtohyggethebritishway.com

- Do you have a Christmas organiser? If not, why? Have a notebook or ringed binder that you can keep all the lists, notes, inspirations you need to plan and have a hyggely Christmas. I have a Cath Kidston paper version kept in a red leather Filofax, plus also a version on Evernote, since I can access that from any of my devices.

Christmas Hygge in the Wide World

Let's start with the widest circle you know.... I've called this chapter Christmas Hygge in the Wide World not because I want you to dive off to Australia, swimming with dolphins and watching Santa coming in on a surfboard, nor do I want you skating off to Japan where they eat KFC as their Christmas dinner of choice (unless you really want to), but to get you thinking about how you can celebrate Christmas in your wider community. This chapter aims to inspire you with ideas for ways to enjoy the holiday season in the towns and countryside. I'd love you to think of ways to celebrate with people beyond your inner circle, as well. There can be a magic in spending time and energy in and around strangers.

In my definition of the wide world I am including shops, theatres, cinemas, markets, day trips, concerts and any place you have to go out of the house to experience the Christmas spirit.

Christmas Shopping? Visit the Shops... but do it with style!

Until The Big Man and his sackful of goodies loses the stranglehold it has on Christmas, then shopping will be an inevitable part of your Christmas experience. You will always have somebody that needs a present buying for them, even if it's only the cat. There can be few nightmares more intense than the panicked feeling of shopping a couple of days before Christmas, the push of the crowds, the rush to find a Perfect Present and at a good price. Quite frankly, I hate shopping in December if it means going to a shopping centre with a list and trying to suit everybody in one day. My feet ache, my head is spinning, my blood sugars plummet down to my boots and I am desperate to find something... anything... for Auntie May who doesn't take baths ever, judging by the smell, and whose last smile happened during Morecambe and Wise's last Live Christmas Show, according to repute. Yes, you love her... but it would actually be easier and kinder to spend time with her instead of trying to find a present.

It has to be done, but there are ways to make the experience a lot happier for all concerned. Here are my top hints.

- Cut the list down. Do you really need to buy presents for everybody on the list? If you can simplify it, the time, energy and money really needed will be decimated and you can concentrate on shopping for pleasure not for duty. I talk about this a lot more in the chapter on wider family and friends.
- Keep your shopping as virtual as possible. A lot of things can be bought online (I am an Amazon Babe, with apologies to all the small businesses I could be buying from) and they will be delivered, gift wrapped if you pay extra, and as early

as the next day for a price. I like to spread the cost of Christmas, so my online shopping starts in September and continues through until December. That way, the cost is spread over four months, not just one.

- Buy chic rather than cheap. Once your list has been streamlined, and you know who you're buying for, ask if they would rather have quantity or quality. A handmade pot from the maker might suit them far better than a mass-produced vase from a department store. Even better, make the buying of the gift part of the present and take the recipient to choose their own gift at a craft fair or gallery. On Christmas Day all you will need is a home-made ticket offering the experience. Make sure to follow up on it, though, or it can be seen as the ultimate miser's solution to gift giving.

- Handmade can also be bought online. Etsy have thousands of makers desperate to sell to you. If you know what you want, the chances are there is someone on Etsy making it. Or buy direct from the craftsperson. Most business-savvy crafters have a website, even if it only links to their Etsy shop. I very often visit craft fairs and just collect the crafts person's cards, then go home and browse at my leisure before buying.

- Make it yourself... but allow enough time. There's very little point in a pieced quilt started on Christmas Eve, but you could assemble a quick collection of baking goodies and a cookie jar mix. I love to make a small gift for the people in my family. I've made mugs, painted boxes (definitely my favourite), sewn cats, knitted dolls…. I usually choose something that I can do for everyone and adapt to different people.

I think I've said…. I'm not a big fan of shopping during December. I would far rather get it done, complete and out of the way so that I can walk around the shops free from any pressure to actually buy anything and free to sit and watch the people walking by.

Visit a Christmas Market

Continental Christmas Markets have become big business in the UK over the past 10 years. It's funny, because we used to have a good history of Christmas markets ourselves. I love a good Christmas market, and I'm happy to wander around the stalls, sipping mulled wine and nibbling on whatever nuts are on sale. You don't even need to travel far now for the full continental hit. Look at the websites of your local cities and towns to see what different style markets different ones offer.

For my continental hit, I travel to Manchester (about 20 miles from where I live) which has the reputation locally for having the biggest and best markets for Christmas, with a good mix of continental stalls and local products. Last year I took my daughter and we cadged a lift off the husband, so I could actually indulge in the mulled cider on offer. And the German beer that I had with my lunch. She was disgusted at me drinking in the street and at lunchtime, but by the time we'd wandered around, had an hour in Waterstones and spent every penny on books, cheese, decorations, chocolate and candles, she was chilled at the idea and has already signed up to coming with me again... even if we did have an hour's wait in Starbucks while the Husband worked his way back into the city after his football. We'll probably take the train this year, and make the journey part of the fun.

Even if you spend not one penny, the sights, sounds, smells and sensual hits in the market will make you feel Christmassy. I buy very few presents in the markets, but I love the experience.

Of course, for the ultimate Christmas Market experience you should visit any one of the many continental markets held abroad. I desperately want to go to Copenhagen at Christmastime to see the markets and the Tivoli. My Daughter's school organised a German trip to see the world-renowned markets in Cologne. She loved the whole experience and never fails to delight in telling me that even Manchester doesn't have markets as good. Harrumph.

The Best Way to Spread Christmas Cheer is Singing Loud for All to Hear.

Yes, it's a quote from Buddy the Elf, but it is quite true. Singing, especially singing in company, is better for your health than yoga, according to one Swedish scientist.[3] There is a power in using your lungs to maximum effect, research to show that your heart beats synchronise and slow in a choir singing together, and just a feeling of enjoyment from natural endorphins rushing through your body that makes singing in the choir better than listening to it. And if you manage to sound good as well... that's just an extra benefit. Heart Research UK used it as a fundraising gimmick one year, asking us to join choirs and sing our hearts out[4].

As a Christmas Choir member, I can vouch for the happy feelings that singing brings on. I always end up promising myself to join a choir for the rest of the year, but I want a choir that doesn't take itself seriously and still uses sheet music for learning the tunes rather than learning by listening (which I can't do!).

Church is a rather good way to experience mass singing with the benefit of being free and providing free child care if you choose carefully. Yes, that's sarcasm, to a degree, but true, since if you

---

[3] http://www.telegraph.co.uk/news/health/10168914/All-together-now-singing-is-good-for-your-body-and-soul.html

[4] https://heartresearch.org.uk/fundraising/singing-good-you

begin attending a church regularly you stand a good chance that they have Sunday Groups of one sort or another for children.

Christmas being a rather special time of year, your local Church will probably have special services on, such as a Festival of Nine Lessons and Carols, or a rather more child-friendly Christingle service that you can attend even if the rest of the year you never darken the door. Our Church expects the numbers to swell at Christmas, judges nobody and reckons that any time spent inside is better than no time at all. We try to be a very child-friendly church as well, so you shouldn't feel awkward even if your baby kicks off. I understand not every church is as welcoming…

If quiet contemplation is more your thing, then Midnight Service/Mass on Christmas Eve may be a better time. Generally, you are guaranteed Silent Night and possibly O Come All You Faithful at this service, with a wide range of carols and styles available. Just look on the Church websites or ask your friends or neighbours to recommend one that might suit.

If you don't have a church or choir nearby, or you have personal objections to religious institutions, you can still get the full singing hit from concerts in your area. Look for ones labelled 'singalong' or run for charity on a small-scale. There's often a ticket price, but that's worth paying to give to charity and enjoy the experience of singing along to a band or choir full-blast.

Liverpool Philharmonic Hall, which is my local large Concert Hall, organise a variety of Christmas concerts, from the Sing-a-long with Santa designed specifically for children and families, to The Spirit of Christmas. Ticket prices vary tremendously, so if one event seems way beyond sensible, then look at another one that may be cheaper. My favourite of the Philharmonic events has to be the annual Christmas Eve screening of *It's A Wonderful Life*, on a large screen while the Wurlitzer organ sinks slowly into the ground after playing the music beforehand. At a price of £10 to £17 per ticket, it's a reasonable charge for a memorable event. I know friends who book it every year. It's their traditional Christmas Eve outing.

For good ideas in your area, use recommendations from friends, scour the websites of local venues or look out on Facebook. Many venues have social media sites and post the latest news on concerts etc there.

If you really have no spare cash, look out for free carol singing in city centres or at local markets. These usually happen around the town Christmas tree, or in the town square. The Salvation Army are infamous for getting out there and playing Christmas carols. If all else fails, give your local Salvation Army office a ring and ask them if they have a timetable planned.

Look out for Local Events

Towns and cities are very media savvy now, so it's always worth checking on the local area website to see what is available. In the local Tourist hot-spots there may well be small festivals or art displays put on throughout Christmas. It's worth keeping an eye out for Makers Markets, coffee shop get-togethers, department store events or anything that tickles your fancy to go to. Combined with coffee and a cake, they make a hyggely day out over the season and might make good presents for the friend who has everything!

Remember that local Stately Homes, whether in the National Trust or not, may run special Christmas events but that these very often carry a premium for being during December. We choose our National Trust moments carefully. Tatton Park[5], owned by the Trust but administered by Cheshire County Council, has loads of events on, but likes to charge well for them. Rufford Old Hall[6], run by volunteers, opens with a range of activities planned for children and a very reasonable entry fee, especially if you are already members of the Trust.

And it's worth looking up other local tourist attractions. Zoos, safari parks and farm parks often stay open all year round, because they have animals to feed. Does your local one run special Santa trails, open a grotto or have lantern displays? Look on their websites to see. For about three years our Santa's Grotto was a trip to Park Hall Farm, Shropshire[7]. With animals, mini vehicles to ride around on and a trip to The Big Man himself, it made for a full day out. We always had to book in advance, just to be sure of getting in, but it was worth it.

We also loved the Santa Specials on the East Lancashire Railways[8]. For a train-mad Thomas the Tank Engine fan, the combination of Santa and Steam was irresistible. If you have a child

---

[5] http://www.tattonpark.org.uk/home.aspx

[6] https://www.nationaltrust.org.uk/rufford-old-hall
[7] http://www.parkhallfarm.co.uk/event/christmas-shropshire-santa-experience/
[88] http://www.eastlancsrailway.org.uk/events-activities/2017/11/santa-specials.aspx

with a particular interest, you can probably find a grotto or event to match.

When all else fails, head for the hills

Everybody needs beauty as well as bread, places to play in and pray in, where nature may heal and give strength to body and soul.

John Muir

www.howtohyggethebritishway.com

At some point in the season it all becomes too much. Too loud, too busy, too full of everything. When that happens, get out. Much of this chapter has been about going places full of Christmas and getting the complete blast of commercialised Christmas. But there is an alternative. Just go and find somewhere that doesn't have music piped over the sound system, that hasn't got Santa swiveling on a timer and booming out **Ho Ho Ho** every 30 seconds. Get out into as close to the wilderness as you can.

For some of us (that includes me) the local park will be far enough. Somewhere where you can still get a hot drink or find a loo when you want it, but also somewhere full of fresh air, quietness and the chance to get your head together. For others, the endless possibilities of experiencing the wild in winter will have them heading for the hills and tramping across paths that, in the depths of summer, never get dry. Both extremes are good.

Hygge relies on getting connected with nature, and that can be as toe-dipping or as full-body immersive as you like. The Outdoor Swimming Society[9] organise festive events around the country. In some places, taking a dip on Christmas Day has become an annual event, with mad men and women taking to the water to enjoy a bracing experience, or to raise funds for charity[10]. Most famous of these is the Peter Pan Cup, which is competed for in the waters of the Serpentine in Hyde Park by members of the swimming club. It's been run since 1864, but in 1904 J M Barrie donated the Cup as a prize and, indeed, presented it himself until the early 1930s. It's cold, but not as cold as Moscow which also boasts a history of Christmas Day swims.

---

[9] https://www.outdoorswimmingsociety.com/

As I was writing this chapter, I posted an article in the Hygge Nook asking if anyone had swum at night and got the response from one member that she swam outside every day. Every day of the year. She said that 15 of them had a pre-Christmas group swim, with a National Trust Turkey lunch afterwards to warm up, but that she had swum throughout December wearing little but a smile and a woolly hat. I wish I could show you her picture, her beaming face is a joy to see!

My immersion in Nature is nowhere near as extreme as that: I would far rather walk in a forest, or stroll along a windy beach. As long as it's somewhere free from canned Christmas music, shops and too many other people I'll be happy. I like getting cold noses, toes and fingers especially if there's a chance of a warm mug of cocoa or glögg at the end. And as with all hygge, the return home to the warmth of a snuggly house makes the experience even more magnificent.

Action!!!

- Wear a smile, don't push, finish as much of your present shopping by November as possible so that your trips in

---

https://www.theguardian.com/lifeandstyle/the-swimming-

December don't rely on finding the perfect gift and can focus on having fun.

- Don't try and do everything at once; you don't have to go everywhere every year. Pick a few ideas for this year and release the rest. Promise yourself to put them top of the list for next Christmas. You may find by then that your priorities have changed and you want to do something else.

I find that Winter wraps me up in that hygge feeling that we have all come to appreciate.

Christiane Bellstedt Myers

www.howtohyggethebritishway.co.uk

- Build in some time to look at nature as well. Get out to the park or to the hills. Some Stately Homes are closed during the Winter, but their grounds stay open. And a beach walk or river-side stroll will always be reenergising. Any fresh air helps to blow the cobwebs away.

Christmas Hygge in the Workplace

Whatever your workplace or office is like the rest of the year, a strange thing seems to happen during the month of December. It's like people who, the rest of the year, keep away from you suddenly find a bonhomie that is missing from their lives and want to be your best friend. Could it be they know you've got their name in the office Secret Santa?

I am not the best qualified to speak of office behaviour or etiquette, since I worked in schools for 20 years and now work in a small 2-person office. Our Secret Santa works very well. I buy him something, and he buys me something back. And since we're even married to each other, we know what each other likes. If you work in a big office, or for a firm split over several floors or sites, then I can't give you advice. I should be writing to you for help!

Different firms have different traditions on when and how much you can decorate a desk for Christmas, from the minimalism of nothing to a free-for-all with tinsel and tack. You'll have to check what your firm likes, but it is worth putting a little something on your desk as a reminder of the good times to be had. I work on the front desk, so I couldn't put too much bling out for Christmas. Last year I was very elegant, with a small tree and a wooden Christmas house.

It was about the only Christmas decorations we did put up in the office, but it was enough to keep me happy. I had to recognise the need to keep the public office looking sensible, mature, ready for work at all times as taking priority over my natural inclination that more (at Christmas) is definitely more.

One hygge nook member described herself as the office 'Christmas Crazy' and said, "Me and the only other Christmas crazy at the Foodbank where I volunteer have been the nominated 'elves' that make Christmas happen every year... from all the decorations, to collecting and wrapping hamper boxes, to organising and shopping and catering for the annual Christmas do....but everything can only go up on a strict date and has to be down again by a strict date..." With some workers channeling The Grinch before his heart grew, this may be the best thing to do. Not everybody will want to join in, or feel able to participate in anything expensive or time-consuming.

If you are a Christmas Crazy, Elf, Fairy or Godmother, then you can do a lot to drag the Spirit of Christmas into the workplace all by yourself. Don't despair if things don't seem hyggely at first, keep going. You are aiming to change a workplace culture that is very deeply ingrained. You will need to use charm, persistence and the conviction of belief to demonstrate that the office is better with cake than without.

Decorate your desk or space

If your desk isn't on public display, and the company allow decorations, then there are so many tasteful things to do. I'm assuming that tinsel is just too in your face here, and that if you're after a hyggely desk, you'd like it to veer more towards the Scandi-chic than tinsel tack.

- Decorate using natural objects. Use rocks, pine cones or small branches of fir to create a bowl-sized display. Have some traditional Christmas nuts, such as brazil or walnuts, and spray them gold.
- A small twig tree with some artificial snow sprayed on it, and cute wooden decorations hung from it can be very effective. For an authentically hygge look, use just red and white as the colour scheme. And, if you're crafty, why not make some felt decorations yourself? Simple stars, tree shapes and

stockings trimmed with ribbon and embroidery are bright and cheery.

- Be the desk that always has a Christmas tin full of biscuits on it. If you're a good baker, then **pebbernodder** are easy to make and smell divine. With a name meaning pepper nuts, they are small enough to enjoy without pigging out and spicy enough to keep you happy. There are several recipes available on the internet, or in many good Scandinavian recipe books.[11][12] They're a traditional Christmas biscuit all over Denmark, Germany and the Netherlands.

---

[11]https://www.amazon.co.uk/d/Books/Scandinavian-Christmas-Trine-Hahnemann/1849491925/ref=sr_1_5?ie=UTF8&qid=1502890328&sr=8-5&keywords=trine+hahnemann is a really good Scandinavian Christmas recipe book.

- If you're not a baker, why not be the Chocolate Elf? Having a small bowl that you keep topped up with a selection of chocolates can make your desk very popular. You don't need to shell out a fortune for Big Names like Roses, Quality Street or Celebrations, try the local discount Supermarkets and see what their chocolates set you back. Or buy sharing bags of Revels and Skittles. The point is not to feed the world, it's to create a hub of chat and sharing at your desk.

- Forced bulbs are very seasonal and often given as presents at this time of year. If you plan ahead (as in September) you can have a few pots of hyacinths ready to go on your desk from the middle of December. Although I always think the blue hyacinths are beautiful and smell divine, a bowl of white hyacinths, with tasteful Christmas additions, could be a brilliant alternative to a Christmas tree. Or go for the amaryllis bulbs that are sold as presents in most supermarkets. Plant one at the start of December and watch it grow! This is also a lovely thing to do after the Christmas break is over and you return to a cold, empty, sad-looking desk. Watching the Amaryllis turn into a Triffid might be the best relaxation you get this January!

- Decorate the plants you have. It doesn't take a lot to stick a few baubles on wire and plant them judiciously among the

---

12   http://nordicfoodliving.com/danish-peppernuts-pebernodder/ has one version of the *pebbernodder* recipe. I'm sure if you know any authentic Danes or

leaves of your Calla lily or spider plant. Or cover the soil with a layer of white (cotton wool, or snow-sprayed moss work well) and use Christmas cake decorations to make your own little scene.

- Use a terrarium to build a snow-globe with no water. With a layer of sand or gravel, a layer of cotton wool snow and an assortment of figures and decorations, you could even keep a flour shaker of artificial snow or glitter next to it and see which of your colleagues just can't resist playing with the snow globe!

Once the desk is decorated, see how far you can push it. Can you put a Christmas throw over your chair? Hang a wreath on your door? At the very least you can Christmas your mugs for the season. Cheap and cheerful Christmas-themed mugs are available in all the supermarkets once Hallowe'en is over, so treat yourself to a couple and make every cup you drink a cup of Christmas love.

Even Computers need to Celebrate

If your job is anything like 50% of my friends (and mine) then you probably spend a fair proportion of your day looking at a computer screen and typing on a keyboard. If company policy allows it, then why not Christmas your computer screen? It only takes a few

Germans, they'll share their family recipe with you!

minutes to find a good image and superimpose a Christmas greeting. The one below was done in 3 minutes while I waited for the kettle to boil.

I used Publisher, but a good online quotes creator programme[13] should have you master of your Christmas Destiny in a few minutes.

And for true Christmas obsessives, you could always fit a set of Christmas keyboard stickers over the letters! Anything with stars or

---

[13] https://quotescover.com/quotes-maker/app/choose-editor2 is my usual one. It's easy and offers a wide range of format choices.

angels would be lovely.[14]

The computer may also be a suitable place to keep a music playlist ready to turn on any chance you get. I have a Christmas playlist that I listen to when I get the chance (ie when nobody is ringing the office or I've finished the dictation for the day). Be aware that if you are playing it for anybody other than your own self (through headphones) then the office may need a PRS certificate.

And the final Computer Christmas idea may sound bizarre, but actually has a practical point as well. Since Christmas and the months immediately following it are peak cold and flu season, it makes sense to disinfect your keys regularly. Using Zoflora[15] gives you the option of choosing from a range of scents that includes hyacinths, summer breeze and (often only available during the winter) a seasonal scent that usually includes cinnamon or ginger. Using a piece of kitchen roll, dampen it slightly with Zoflora, making sure that any excess liquid is carefully squeezed out and then gently wipe over the keys with the cloth. Most of the germs should be wiped away and a waft of Christmassy scent should be present for a few hours at the very least.

---

[14] https://www.amazon.co.uk/Christmas-Protactor-Decoration-Keyboard-Decoration/dp/B00PIK9Q5W/ref=sr_1_4?ie=UTF8&qid=1502832055&sr=8-4&keywords=christmas+computer+keyboard+stickers features a beautiful rooftop at night scene. It's for Mac keyboards, so you might need to mess with the stickers a little to make them fit.

[15] http://www.zoflora.co.uk/products

Bring in seasonal baked goods for Fika

Let's Fika!

Meaning "let's get together over coffee, eat some cake and have a chat"

www.howtohyggethebritishway.com

Fika is the Swedish word for a proper coffee break. It's a good time to stop for a few minutes, talk to your colleagues and find out more about what makes them tick. I don't expect, or even ask, that you get the whole office stopping to share a stollen bite or a mincemeat puff, but that you set the example and see who follows you. Bring in a plateful of tasty miniature goodies, take the time to make yourself a proper coffee, or a pot of tea, and sit either at the staffroom table or at your desk to enjoy a quiet oasis in a busy life. Invite one friend, ask another person the next day and the next. Fika (like hygge) isn't something you try once and give up on. It takes determination. And you have that aplenty.

To widen the Fika circle, you could try bringing in a weekly Christmas cake. I don't mean a great big heavy fruitcake that costs a fortune and weighs you down on the bus. I mean a sponge cake, or a lemon drizzle cake, or a chocolate roll. Use your imagination and dress it up a little to be more Christmassy (a simple holly leaf or robin should be enough with a sprinkling of icing sugar) and you have the start of a lovely tradition. If anybody else offers to bring in a cake, bite their hand off. Hygge happens when everybody plays a part, and a good volunteer should never be discouraged.

You need breaks to make it these days...

In the mid-eighties, when Gordon Gecko reigned supreme, lunch was for wimps. Not so nowadays. Your lunch break can be a time when you recharge yourself mentally and physically. Use your time allowance, and use it well. You might find a walk is what you need. Get out of the office and go searching for Christmas. If you work in the middle of a town or city, you won't have to look far. If you work on a business park or in a skyscraper, then finding the Christmas love might take a little longer. Look harder, it will be there, in a card on someone's desk, the sound of Christmas music being piped in the elevator or in the glimpse of a robin flying past the window.

If you are lucky enough to work near a park or an open space then you can enjoy the winter at its best. Frosty walks, feeding ducks at the local pond or searching out red berries in hedgerows and gardens can all give you a focused and grounded feeling. Christmas, as the Grinch finally found out, doesn't come out of a box. Finding signs of the turning year in the world around you is a very real way of keeping in touch with the changing seasons.

Grab a small craft project and get a little done every day. Something small and portable like an embroidery, a sketchbook or a crochet coaster could be almost finished after a week of downtime. And creating something, even if just for 10 minutes, will give you a great feeling of accomplishment.

Use the lunchbreak to build a friendship. Invite somebody you ordinarily don't get a chance to talk to much and share a coffee with them, or buy lunch from the same sandwich shop. Use December to build a bond over the common love of Christmas. Talk to them, ask them about their life. If you, like me, usually struggle to make small talk then remember it is easier to listen than to talk. Have a list of questions in mind, about their life, home or ambitions. Start off impersonal and build up to the deep questions of Life, the Universe and everything.

What happens at the Office Party...

Stays at the Office party? I'm not a big fan of massive parties with lots of noise or drinking. One gives me a headache the other.... also gives me a headache. I like smaller groups, it seems more hyggely to me when you can talk and listen to each other.

On the rare occasion that I've been out on a Christmas Do I find it much easier to circulate and talk to people with a clear head. I like table hopping, and have been known to find a way to sit at every table and say hi. That way I have a room full of friends rather than strangers and always someone to dance with. The clear head also helps in knowing what you got up to during the party. No morning after worries for me, thank you very much.

But I appreciate that the feeling of freedom given by a large office party is irresistible to other people. If they're your thing, then go. Enjoy the night and **carpe diem** (as the saying goes, although really here it should be more **carpe nox**) with no regrets and no guilt.

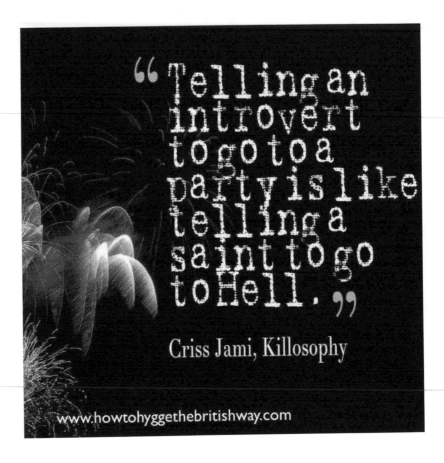

" Telling an introvert to go to a party is like telling a saint to go to Hell. "

Criss Jami, Killosophy

www.howtohyggethebritishway.com

I prefer a smaller group, perhaps just a department or even just a few work colleagues getting together for drinks and a meal after work. There's a line between work and home-life that we tend not to want to cross, so that we keep them separate. Sometimes that's because you don't particularly like your colleagues. Sometimes it's to do with wanting a private life. Whatever your reason, you are entitled to feel like that. But if you never make a link with colleagues, even if only over the small stuff, then it makes being a cog in the machine that much harder. It is easier to be a part of a team when the team know enough about each other to appreciate why different people feel like they do about certain things.

If you really don't like the Office Party, then hold out and push for a smaller event. Ask people on your floor to come out with you, ask them home, invite them for coffee, go for a meal. Share some of your life with them. To build hygge in the workplace you will need to build links between people. Start small, build your team slowly. Appreciate that both extroverts and introverts want to celebrate, it's just they do it differently. Giving people the chance to join in at their own level may be the best thing you encourage in your work situation.

So, Secret Santa... or blind date?

I am a mad Christmas fan, but I have qualms about Secret Santa. Done correctly, it can be a happy way to show friendship and respect for a colleague.... Done incorrectly it is a cause of embarrassment and an unnecessary expense at an already-stretched time.

In any case, participation must be voluntary and the figure set low enough for anyone to join in yet high enough to make finding something worthwhile possible. You're not after a massive present, but a token of appreciation and friendship.

That token should also maintain each person's dignity and pride. At one work location I know of, the Secret Santa went completely out of hand, with a totally unsuitable gift being presented in public to the Boss.

It caused merriment amongst some of the staff and deep embarrassment amongst others, who thought that the item in question had a definite NSFW[16] warning on it. Never get lewd, crude or suggestive in a Secret Santa in the workplace. Even if you know them very well, save **that** present for a personal moment.

It can be difficult to buy for someone you know only professionally, especially on a limited budget, so it's often easier to stick to generic presents: chocolates, toiletries, candles or a bottle of wine. It's harder to find a personal present for a colleague unless you actually make the effort to ask about them, what they like or dislike, what food they love, what activities they do. It can be lovely as the recipient to know that somebody has taken the time to find out something about you and to be given something that won't just go in the charity bag.

I love giving things that will be used up... I was going to write comestibles, but that ignores things like candles and flowers that won't last forever. Any food is good, especially if you know the recipient will like it. Try the German discount stores for things like biscuits or chocolate in cute tins. I have at least 3 musical tins from Aldi, simply because they had **pebbernodder** in and each played a different Christmas tune. Alcohol (think miniatures for a reasonable price) or a quirky foodstuff such as tea or flavoured coffee works well also. Or give a gift that will last for a while, such as flower bulbs or seeds.

---

[16] Not Suitable For Work

Search online for something suitable. If the recipient likes a particular animal, pop group or film star then it might be that you can get them a coaster, a tea towel or a poster with that on. Getting a guinea pig-mad person a guinea pig keyring is just another way of showing that you actually put some thought into the gift, and didn't just grab the first thing in the supermarket.

Look at the role that the person holds in the company and try to build a gift around that. The receptionist at one school was also the Chief Dinner Lady who stood out on the yard 5 days a week. For her Secret Santa gift, I bought 5 cheap handwarmers (approximately £1 each!) and wrapped them up separately with a chocolate bar each, labelled Monday, Tuesday etc. She really didn't expect them, but she used them during the winter, so I reckon that was a useful present to get her. You could try notebooks, pens or pencils, sticky notes in different shapes, window stickers, computer decals or anything useful in their role.

Wrap it beautifully in tissue paper and then a brown paper sack, label with care and let them be delighted with a secret Santa gift that won't have them hanging their head in shame.

Address the senses as you address the envelopes

Christmas is a time for sensory overload: there are so many smells, sounds and textures around to delight, so why should the office be left out? It only takes a few minutes to find ways to engage all the senses, so give it a go.

- Use a diffuser or spray essential oils mixed with water and vodka to delight the nose. Using cinnamon and vanilla relaxes: ginger invigorates. Suggestions for room scents are available online, but I like to make my own air freshener using a recipe from The Autumn House[17] by Alison May. Simply mix 5 drops of frankincense, 3 drops of fir balsam and 4 drops of neroli with a cup of distilled water and a cup of vodka. Shake well and store in a small spray bottle.

- Use a throw or a cushion to bring in the sense of touch. Contrasting textures such as velvet or corduroy can be good. As can keeping rocks or pieces of wood on the desk. The contrasting textures stimulate the brain, and help people think.

- Keep the office clutter free, but indulge in works of art to stimulate the sense of sight. At Christmas-time you will have access to one of the most undervalued artworks ever... the Christmas Card. Display some on your desk or why not have everybody bring in a Christmas card each that you display as part of a mass washing line along one wall.

---

[17]
https://www.amazon.co.uk/dp/B07579F4WS/ref=sr_1_1?ie=UTF8&qid=150451 7877&sr=8-1&keywords=the+autumn+house

- To give your ears a gentle soundtrack, and as long as the office is legally able to, then playing certain kinds of Christmas music can be helpful. This is not the time to have Slade or Wizzard on endless repeat, but choosing some mellow jazz or soft classical could be a good idea. I love the Carol Symphony by Victor Hely-Hutchinson, or the Pasadena Roof Orchestra's Christmas Album. You're after music that won't take over the office, but will make people smile when they hear it first.
- Finally: taste… this is easy. Just get the best bakers you know to keep up an endless stream of cinnamon rolls, **peppernodder** or other deliciously spicy food.

Build in the Altruism

The office that works for charity together works well together. Charitable giving is a traditional part of Christmas. From early times, helping people who have less than us has been a duty of most major religions and most irreligious people as well.

The business men who turned up outside Scrooge's office felt the need to help others. That need never goes, so why not build up the hygge of the office by working together as a team to raise some money for charity?

> " **A few of us are endeavouring to raise a fund to buy the Poor some meat and drink, and means of warmth. We choose this time, because it is a time, of all others, when Want is keenly felt, and Abundance rejoices.** "
>
> Charles Dickens, A Christmas Carol

www.howtohyggethebritishway.co.uk

You want quick, easy and simple ideas for money raising at Christmas. Now is not the time for a major sponsored event or a weekend of jelly-bathing. Given the packed timetables and account books of a majority of people at Christmas, you're really after things that take virtually no time and add no major pressure.

One hygge nook member said that her office take part in the Christmas Jumper day. For a donation you can wear a jumper with elves, Santa or a big red Rudolph on ALL DAY LONG. Christmas

Jumper Day in the UK is run on behalf of Save the Children, but there's no law saying that as an office you can't choose a charity dear to your heart. It would be a fitting way to remember a lost colleague, or to highlight a cause that means a lot to the company.

Perhaps you could start a small change jar, and leave it out on a desk for people to drop their pennies and change in. It does mean someone taking charge of it, emptying it regularly and taking the cash to the bank when it's time to change it up for big money. Every penny counts, so even a few coins can soon add up.

If everybody is in agreement, do without Christmas cards in the office. Everybody brings just one (see Address the Senses above) which goes on display and then donates the money they've saved to a charity of their choice. It also cuts back on waste, so there's a win-win situation.

It's always easier to get money off people when they're getting something in return. Perhaps a dedicated baker could hold a cake sale, or a cookie sale with all profits going to charity. Some hospitals and hospices sell decorations to fundraise at this time of year. If you know anybody connected to your local hospice, it is well worth asking them. They may be glad of another outlet raising money for them.

Ask the company bosses for a donation of a prize and hold a prize draw within the company. I think if tickets are being sold to the general public you need a licence, but for internal prize draws with an element of skill you don't need a licence (UK law only). Have some element of skill such as a card designing contest, a short Christmas quiz or wordsearch or a slogan competiton, charge a small fee for entering and appoint an impartial judge.

Keep people involved and up to date on how the fundraising has gone. And keep it relaxed. You're not aiming to raise as much as Children In Need, just to have some fun while also helping out a local cause.

And don't let any hygge fade after Christmas. Keep up the friendship, build the bridges, work on being happy in the workplace. Smiles are contagious, so see how far yours can go.

Action!!!

- Find out company policy on decorating, parties, Secret Santa well in advance of December. Start planning your preferred alternative, if you have to.
- Write a list of small actions you can do to boost hygge in the workplace. Whether you work with the Grinch or Mr Fezziwig, set them in motion and spread the happiness.

Stay positive and happy. Work hard and don't give up hope. Be open to criticism and keep learning. Surround yourself with happy, warm and genuine people.

Tena Desae

www.howtohygge
thebritishway.co.uk

- Find a Christmas buddy in the office or online who will share your love of Christmas with you.

The Celebrations of Winter: Thanksgiving, Hanukkah, Diwali and Winter Solstice.

In 1997 Birmingham Council used the word Winterval[18] to describe a season of events that included Diwali, Christmas, Chinese New Year and New Year's Eve for marketing purposes. Very soon the cry went up that Winterval had been dreamt up by some atheist determined to cut Christ out of Christmas. Although Birmingham Council soon stopped using the word, it's a testament to its usefulness that Winterval still persists as both an acceptable term to cover a multitude of festivals that all take place during the winter season and a derogatory way to say that the Christian element of Christmas is being underplayed. Sometimes it's used for both purposes in the same sentence.

In our multicultural society it really does make sense to know about other people's faiths and festivals as it gives us another common bond. It also helps to know which ways they are best celebrated, when they begin and end and what greetings are associated with them. During my short career as a primary school teacher it was interesting to see how our perception of these festivals changed from something that 'other people' celebrated (back in the 80s) to something that is celebrated with other people. I think a lot of

---

[18] https://en.wikipedia.org/wiki/Winterval

nursery and reception classes find the autumn term an ideal time to do celebrations just because from the end of October there are so many chances and ways to learn about ourselves and others through faith and secular celebrations.

I have tried, in this short chapter, to include an overlook at different celebrations from Halloween to Twelfth Night. That covers the period from October 31st to January 6th. I've mainly concentrated on the feasts that celebrate light, home and family, since those are the ones that usually have the most hyggely celebrations to me. I love anything that is about having special meals together (Hanukkah), eating sweets without guilt (Diwali) or asks me to light even more candles to beat the darkness outside (Winter Solstice). I couldn't include every one, so apologies if I've missed your favourite feast out. I've just included a few facts about the most common celebrations of the wintertime, and a couple of ways to celebrate them. More resources are listed, of course, in the Resources chapter at the end of the book.

Halloween

Celebrated on 31st October and meaning the eve of All Hallows Day (All Saints Day), Halloween has been celebrated in Britain for as long as anybody knows. It marks the start of the Christian period known as Allhallowtide, a time for remembering the saints, the dead and the martyred. In Mexico, the season is known as The Day of

The Dead, and marked by parties and celebration parades, or by visiting the graves of family, or both.

Both celebrations mark a meeting of the physical world and the beyond or otherworld. They became tied in to divination, communing with the 'otherside', or thoughts of death. Of course, this is the side that appears most in modern Halloween movies, with ghosts and spirits making excellent movie fodder to scare the unwary.

PEOPLE VALUE HALLOWEEN, LIKE VALENTINE'S DAY, BECAUSE THEY CAN TELL THEMSELVES THAT IT'S NOT MERELY SECULARIZED BUT ACTUALLY SECULAR, WHICH IS TO SAY, NOT CHRISTIAN, JEWISH, HINDU OR MUSLIM.

Amity Shlaes

www.howtohyggethebritishway.com

Halloween celebrates using the fruit of the season. Apples, nuts, squash and pumpkins are all available at the end of October, and carving a large pumpkin to make a face or a picture lantern can be a good activity for a cold Sunday afternoon. Don't forget to use the flesh for soup, pumpkin pie or to thicken a stew.

Shops get in their Halloween decorations as soon as the Back to School displays are gone. In the UK that usually means a whole load of skeletons, black witches, orange plastic pumpkins and anything that creeps, crawls, moans or jumps in dummy form, complete with batteries and fake cobwebs.

To celebrate Halloween tastefully in your house, decorate the windows with squashes. Last year I had a variety of squash on the window sill, and they stayed there for quite a few weeks. With fairy lights strung around them, they made an easy and cheap display that could legitimately count as Halloween and Thanksgiving. Eat by candlelight, tell ghost stories or just listen to the wind. There are few things more hyggely than time inside on a night when others are walking around in the wind.

Halloween in my childhood meant toffee apples, colouring books and sweets midweek. We lived on a main road, so there was no chance of Trick or Treating and the only Halloween party I went to, I cried.

Bonfire Night

Remembering a failed assassination attempt 500 years after the event through fireworks and bonfires may seem a tad strange, but Bonfire Night is a peculiarly British evening, celebrated on November 5th and remembered through the rhyme,

> Remember, remember the fifth of November
>
> Gunpowder, treason and plot.
>
> I see no reason why gunpowder treason
>
> Should ever be forgot.

Sadly, the rhyme is being forgotten, like many old, traditional rhymes, and the history behind it sliding into obscurity.

The whole story of Guy Fawkes' attempt to blow up the Houses of Parliament complete with the King who was there to open it has a thick layer of myth built around it. Despite Guy Fawkes being the name we all know, it wasn't his idea, he was only a paid hitman. For whatever reason connected to the fun of fireworks, bonfires and the macabre act of throwing a guy on the fire, celebration of the day itself has persisted, although in recent times it has been overshadowed by the more commercialised and Americanised Halloween.

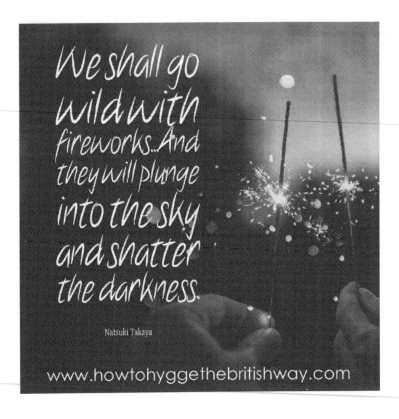

We shall go wild with fireworks...And they will plunge into the sky and shatter the darkness.

Natsuki Takaya

www.howtohyggethebritishway.com

Strangely, the commemoration of Bonfire Night was enshrined in UK law until 1859, when the law was repealed. It's still marked with firework displays by many councils in the UK and in Lewes they still have a traditional parade every year during which effigies of public figures are paraded through the streets, along with 17 burning crosses to remember the local martyrs, before being burnt on one of five bonfires in the town.

Bonfire food includes anything warm and eaten outside, with toffee apples, sausages and hot dogs, baked potatoes and warm soup topping the list. I have a fondness for bonfire toffee[19], a traditional make at this time of the year in the North of England. As recently as the 1960s there was still a tradition of it being made and handed out to the children who came asking for a penny for the Guy. Perhaps there's always been an element of Trick or Treat going on. I'm also partial to a good slice of Parkin[20], a traditional oatmeal and treacle cake that is really best made a couple of weeks before being eaten as it improves with keeping, becoming softer and easier to eat.

Bonfire Night can be a hard one to celebrate at home since health and safety as well as cost has made attending the large organised displays a better choice than holding one in your back garden, but at the very least a few sparklers will add a glow to the night. As always, be safe and sure to keep anything hot away from little ones or animals. And come back to a late supper of tomato soup, hotdogs and cheese toasties for a night to remember.

If you're housebound, then a pack of indoor fireworks might be an idea. These small pellets and paper twists sit on a plate and use the magic of science to produce small explosions, unfurling snakes of ash and smells that will keep younger children happy whilst also keeping them warm and cosy inside. Finish off with parkin and a good pot of tea.

---

[19] https://en.wikipedia.org/wiki/Bonfire_toffee
[20] https://en.wikipedia.org/wiki/Parkin_(cake)

Diwali[21]

Celebrated by Hindus, Jains, Sikhs and some Buddhists, this festival of lights celebrates the triumph of good over evil, light over darkness and love over hate. That seems like a good reason to celebrate. It's a five-day festival, during which lights are lit and the community celebrate. People clean their houses from top to bottom, buy new clothes to wear especially for the festival and make lots and lots of food. Different regions and religions have different stories and myths associated with the festival, but they all essentially focus on light and peace.

If you have a Hindi friend, it is good to get them to explain the season in more detail and show you what they do to mark the event. Look out for local events in the papers as well. Some authorities hold Diwali celebrations to which all are welcome. Especially of note: Trafalgar Square[22] have had a Diwali celebration for the past couple of years. If you can get to one, it's a good idea to experience Diwali with other people, so that you can talk to them and ask them what it means to them.

To mark Diwali in a non-Hindu household, especially with children, it's a good idea to focus on one story connected to the festival. Perhaps the story of Rama and Sita is a good starting point. Look at

---

21 https://en.wikipedia.org/wiki/Diwali
22 https://www.london.gov.uk/events/2017-10-15/diwali-festival-2017

websites, watch the clips and talk about how similar or different it is from the festivals that you celebrate.

Hanukkah (or Chanukah)[23]

This is a Jewish festival commemorating the rededication of the Temple in Jerusalem. It's an 8-day festival, marked by the lighting of candles on a Menorah. Eight candles signify the eight days that the sacred oil (only enough for one day in reality) lasted, while fresh oil was blessed and dedicated. It's also called the Feast of Dedication or the Festival Lights and can happen anytime between November and the end of December. It often seems to fall in or near to Christmas, perhaps because we are on the look-out for lights at Christmastime.

Surprisingly for many people who link Christmas and Hanukkah, Hanukkah isn't marked as a religious or Sabbath-like holiday, so many Jews will go to work or school during the day before coming home to light the candles and say the prayers around the family table. Small gifts are exchanged and money is often given to the children. Jewish faith schools often break up for the week, though.

Since it isn't one of the major holy festivals, Hanukkah is a very home-based time. It would be good to ask a Jewish friend to explain

---

[23] https://en.wikipedia.org/wiki/Hanukkah

what the festival means to them, and to show how they celebrate it. For Christians, it is always worth remembering that Hanukkah was one of the festivals Jesus would have known, although it was celebrated slightly differently in his time.

Because of the emphasis on oil, fried food is popular at this time. Potato latkes and donuts are very popular. If you'd like a taste of Hanukkah in your own home, try making some fried food and playing dreidel... you can find some helpful rules on the website in the references below[24]. And for an interesting take on whether a Christian should learn about and mark Hanukkah, there are links to a couple of diverse blogposts in the Resources section.

Thanksgiving

A public holiday celebrated on the fourth Thursday of November in the USA and on the second Monday in October by Canadians, Thanksgiving's US roots date back to 1621, when the Pilgrim Fathers invited the local Wampanoag tribe to a harvest feast as a thanksgiving for teaching them to grow corn, beans and squash, catch the local fish and collect seafood. In 1863 Abraham Lincoln declared the last Thursday in November as Thanksgiving Day[25], but

---

[24] https://holidappy.com/holidays/Understanding-Hanukkah-For-Non-Jews

[25] http://www.telegraph.co.uk/news/0/thanksgiving-day-whats-the-history-of-the-holiday-and-why-does-the-us-celebrate-pilgrim-fathers/

Franklin D Roosevelt changed it to the fourth Thursday because some years November had five Thursdays.

More people celebrate Thanksgiving in the USA than celebrate Christmas, and they do it with a full Turkey dinner. They dress the house, get family together, and watch traditional TV including the Macy's Parade in New York and American Football games.

The holiday marks the Big Start of **the** Holiday Season in the USA, and is followed by Black Friday in many shops, with big sales and savings to be made. As a counter-act to such blatant commercialisation, several societies organise Buy Nothing Days and push for people to spend the weekend with their families rather than in the mall.

Canadian thanksgiving[26] dates back to Martin Frobisher in 1578. He wanted to give thanks for his safe arrival in the New World. Declared a National Holiday in 1879, the date was set in October because the origins are tied more closely to a traditional Harvest festival than the USA Thanksgiving, where the date is tied to the date that the Pilgrim Fathers landed. The food eaten seems remarkably similar... turkey, squash and pies for dessert.

---

[26] http://www.thecanadianencyclopedia.ca/en/article/thanksgiving-day/

Advent

A Holy season in the Christian Church year. In fact, Advent is the first season of the liturgical (Church) year, and is a holy season of preparation. It used to be a season of penance, repentance and fasting, but very little of that survives even amongst strong Christians today.

It exists on two levels: as a period of preparation for celebrating the birth of Christ at Christmas and as a period of reflection and preparation for the expected Second Coming. I quite like that idea, that we're celebrating past and future in one season. The holiest I've ever been at advent is to follow a bible-reading course, but as a mother and now as a worker, my time in December doesn't usually allow for long, multi-questioned studies. My daily dose of bible inspiration now comes in the form of an advent calendar with a bible verse for each day. Short, sharp and just enough to muse on as I race around.

Advent is celebrated well throughout the Scandinavian countries, often with little packages for each child every day and a traditional advent wreath marking all four Sundays. I will be talking more about Advent as part of the House Elf chapter.

The Feast Of St Nicholas

December 6th is St Nicholas' Day[27]. As the traditional origin of Santa Claus, it is worth taking time to remember this Bishop of Myra as a charitable man, a generous giver and the source of several Christmas traditions… not least, that of hanging stockings by the fire!

His feast day is widely celebrated all over Europe, with presents left in shoes or stockings, or a visit from St Nicholas himself. The day has the nickname "Little Christmas" and gives children a chance to exercise patience for the rest of the month. St Nick only leaves presents for the good children, bad children get left a switch (a cane to be beaten with) or a visit from Krampus as well.

December 6th is an ideal date for Christians to celebrate, since it gives children something to look forward to in the run up to Christmas and doesn't need to be a big deal. I used to mark it with sweets, St Nicholas crafts and a special watching of Fred Claus, as a suitably childish version of the origin story. I still like to watch it now, for the moral of the story and the soundtrack as well as Kevin Spacey in full evil mode as the Man Who Bans Christmas.

The traditional food of the feast is speculatius, a spiced biscuit shaped in special moulds. You should be able to find some in most

---

[27] http://www.stnicholascenter.org/pages/home/

supermarkets, or you could try to make your own using an internet recipe.

The Winter Solstice

Celebrated in the Northern Hemisphere on the shortest day of the year, the Solstice is an astronomical moment marking the turn from days shortening to days lengthening. Although linked to paganism and druidism, marking significant changes in the natural cycle is as old as, well, mankind. So many aspects of the traditional solstice celebrations have been taken over as part of our Christmas celebration, it's difficult to isolate anything that is now specifically Solstice alone: bringing in the evergreens, lighting candles, the Yule log in the fire, feasts, mistletoe. We use the traditional methods to celebrate Solstice but many call it Christmas.

Perhaps it's worth making a special effort on the shortest day to mark the moment. Turn off all the lights in the house first, then gather around the dark table, light a candle for dinner even if you don't usually, tell ghost stories and mark the night that is the traditional start of Winter. I love the book, **The Dark is Rising** by Susan Cooper, a children's book set in mid-winter. I wish I could recommend the film version, but somebody messed with it and completely changed the storyline.

Eating a Christmas Log cake for Solstice would also be a good way to mark the feast. The log-shaped, chocolate cakes we now eat are an homage to the large trunks of trees that were taken into the great halls of the past and burned throughout the season as a source of warmth and light.

And bring in some greenery. Buy (or find) some mistletoe to hang in the entrance and tell the story of Balder the Beautiful, or bring in some ivy, holly and green branches. They do decorate a room beautifully, and add a layer of scent to your house.

New Year's Eve

New Year's Eve is traditionally a bigger celebration in Scotland than Christmas. Called Hogmanay, it's marked by parties and fireworks. Edinburgh kicks off their celebrations with a torchlight procession, while people the world over sing the song, Auld Lang Syne, written down by the Scottish poet Robert Burns. Auld Lang Syne roughly translates as "For Old Time's Sake."

Should auld acquaintance be forgot,
And never brought to mind?
Should auld acquaintance be forgot,
And auld lang syne·

For auld lang syne, my jo,
For auld lang syne,
We'll tak a cup o' kindness yet,
For auld lang syne,

And there's a hand, my trusty fiere!
And gie's a hand o' thine!
And we'll tak a right guid willy
waught,
For auld lang syne·

www.howtohyggethebritishway.co.uk

An important tradition for Scots is first-footing, where the first person to enter a house after midnight should be a tall, dark man who brings a gift of coal, shortbread or finest malt whisky. My husband's childhood was spent next door to a lovely old Scottish lady and every year she would send the poor man chosen to first-foot outside, coatless, ten minutes before midnight where he would wait, anxiously awaiting the chimes of Big Ben to be able to knock, be welcomed in and finally... finally... get warm again.

New Year's Eve in our household is spent at home. My teenage years were spent working behind a bar, so the parties hold no thrill for me. We have a Chinese takeaway, watch a film (usually one of our Christmas presents) and toast in the New Year with coke, beer, cider or Buck's Fizz. We know how to live large (not).

Epiphany

The Feast of the Epiphany, or Twelfth Night, marks the end of modern Christmas. In fact, with modern Christmas starting at the beginning of November in shops and taking over the TV schedules from the first of December, many people seem nowadays to want to forget that Christmastide as a Holy Christian season lasts until February 2nd.

Having a season of feasting very nicely marked off with another, final, feast is a good idea. It's like a full stop at the end of the thing. You've partied, drunk and eaten for two weeks, now it's time to stop. Its roots only date back to the 4th Century, but it is well celebrated in Spanish speaking and Orthodox church traditions.

Most people who celebrate have some sort of a cake or tart. In

France, it's a Galette des Rois[28], filled with almond frangipane and hiding a small charm called the fève inside. The lucky person who has the fève inside their slice becomes King or Queen for the night and gets a crown to wear.

Since the day marks the traditional date set aside to remember the visit of the Wise Men to Jesus, there are quite a few celebrations connected to the Magi and Epiphany held around the world.

In Cologne, in Germany, special processions are held in and around the Cathedral. Legend has it that the Three Kings relics are there, in a gilded shrine, and at Epiphany groups of three men or children wander around from house to house, singing. They also chalk up CMB on the wall or above the door. Easy to remember as Caspar, Melchior and Balthazaar the letters actually stand for 'Christus Mansionem Benedicat' and mean 'May Christ Bless this House'.

Epiphany is traditionally the day to have all the Christmas decorations down by, in the UK, and my mother used to take any fresh greenery into the garden to burn it.

To celebrate Epiphany at home, why not hold an end-of-Christmas ceremony: take down all the decorations, put away the Christmas mugs and give the house a good clean. Then, as a family, gather

---

28   http://www.telegraph.co.uk/foodanddrink/recipes/9780514/Baking-club-French-Epiphany-cake-recipe.html

around the table and talk over your favourite moments of that year. Light a candle (or two), drink spiced apple and eat a cake made specially for the day.

There you have it! The celebrations closest to Christmas. It's good to know who is celebrating and why. For a full list of celebrations, and useful information on how and why they are celebrated, may I suggest the Interfaith Network list of seasonal festivals?[29] It covers far more faiths than I have foolishly tried to include here, and in greater depth with links through to further research.

Action!!!

- Pick a couple of the festivals to research each year. You can learn much in a dedicated internet trawl.

- Ask any friends of different faiths to explain what they do and why they do it.

- Picture books about all the religious festivals can be found in libraries and online. They give an easy way into understanding other faiths for a child.

---

[29] https://www.interfaith.org.uk/resources/religious-festivals

Christmas Hygge with your Wide Circle of Family and Friends

Christmas: Season of peace and goodwill to all men, but that might not include your Brother-in-law who is a chauvinist idiot, or the neighbour whose idea of a Silent Night is to get drunk and bawl it out in the early hours of Christmas morning when it has already taken you five hours to talk the children into getting some sleep before Santa comes.

According to the UK charity, Relate, in 2011 over 68% of respondents to a survey expected to argue at some time over the Christmas season, with personality clashes being cited as a major cause of the problem. Christmas is a strange creature: we take time off work to close ourselves up in the house with too much food, too much booze, several generations packed in, a TV system that has too much choice at the same time as having nothing on to watch and the added excitement of new stuff, new distractions and new anxieties and then we expect it to be happy.

We must be fools.

For Christmas celebrations with our wider circle of family and friends to be full of hygge, I think we need to release many of the excessive expectations that we hold. We need to lower the bar, basically. We are deluged by a tidal wave of adverts, magazines, books (excluding this one, obviously!), social media and movies that all portray the idealised perfect family Christmas. That's the one where everybody is full of joy, where nobody ever argues except as a plot device, where the glasses are clean, the Christmas tree never tips over because the cat has climbed up into it and any elderly relatives are as cool as Judi Dench and Pierce Brosnan, exuding charm and a nice line in childcare.

I'm as big a sucker for the Christmas editions of home-style magazines as the next person. I used to buy every single version of them, whether country-home or industrial chic. I loved (and still do) looking into other people's homes, and seeing what the latest fad for trees or turkey or door wreaths was. I have a shelf of A4 journals filled with pictures that I've cut out through the years and stuck in. What I find interesting is that over the years my style has evolved into a distinct and defined style rather than a mish-mash of colours and styles. It's as if I needed to spend time looking at everything to be able to say now "This is my style." and know what I mean. But I digress. We'll talk about home decorating styles in the next chapter.

Real Christmas in the real world isn't about creating a picture-perfect celebration: that's just not possible. It never existed, and it never will. What you have to work on creating is a celebration that is good enough. Let go of the aspirations and let your ambition simply be to be **good enough**, no guilt allowed. I'm not telling you to do without the books and magazines: I find them a useful way to bring Christmas cheer into even the smallest room in the house, but rather to look at them with a clear mind. Remember that the pictures have been set up in July by a trained professional, that the food has been designed by a home economist who has a wealth of experience at his or her beck and call, and that it is all designed to hit your sweet spot. Instead, go back to your ideal Christmas list. What is it that makes the celebration for you? What do **you** want out of Christmas?

Spending Time With Your Extended Family

At some point over the Christmas season the chances are that you will meet up with your extended family. Whether that's a one-day thing, or a few days staying over in one home or another, the pressures of Christmas, over-expectation, having more people in one house than it can reasonably hold, over-eating, alcohol and tiredness can all add up to a dangerous powder keg of emotion.

In many families, there will be three or more generations all getting together for a celebration sometime over Christmas. In my own childhood family there were four siblings, plus Mum, Dad and Nan who lived with us, a number which only expanded with every marriage, baby and circumstance so that, from a manageable 10 we became 20 and this year we are planning a meal for 31 altogether. Our nickname for our family was Rent-a-mob, and we're not getting any fewer in number.

Up until last year we tried to get altogether, in a single house. It meant crowded tables, a busy week of preparation for the host that year, division of labour and cost to keep it fair and a need for a lot of patience on everybody's part to keep the day calm. Fortunately, everybody lives within a 10-mile radius, so there was no extra housekeeping, finding of beds and rooms and desperate attempt to get to the bathroom before someone else to get ready in time to put the turkey in. There had to be a breaking point, and mine was eating my whole Christmas dinner off a plate precariously balanced as I was shoe horned between my Mother and Sister in Law in a too-small room. Last year I refused point blank to go. Christmas has to be different this year.

In smaller, more manageable families, the tradition of getting together on Christmas day is a lovely one. Sharing a great feast together, building relationships that will last forever and having memories that will shine in the darker days of life must be good…. Mustn't it?

Well, realistically, family events in and around Christmas won't all be plain sailing. People are people and they don't always get on. With alcohol, Christmas worries and indigestion, any existing worries can soon be amplified into a major argument. The best ways to deal with this? I don't know: families are very individual and you need to think about your own circumstances to smooth the path as much as possible. Here, with hopes that it is useful, is a list of my top advice for a Big Family Christmas.

- Plan as much as possible ahead of time. Draw up a spread sheet with expected arrival and departure times of any guests staying, cooking and baking times for any big feasts involved and, yes, even housekeeping tasks so that you know when you should really clean the toilets, brush the kitchen and wipe over the sides. Display it somewhere prominent and don't say no if anyone asks to help, just point them towards a task.

- Make a list and check it twice. Check on things like plates, knives, spoons well in advance. Mugs are a good one, since they have a habit of going missing. If you're expecting a large crowd, give everyone their own mug and put them in charge of looking after it themselves. Check you have enough early enough in the month and you can either buy or borrow extras without a Christmas Eve panic.

- Have Hygge space available for different generations. Your Great Grandma will need a chair to sleep in, your teenagers will need a den to hide in and your bossy Sister in Law will need a space to call her own where she can take charge. I don't have any bossy S-i-Ls (that means it's probably me in our family) but I do know people who have, and they usually put them in charge of a whole area like childcare, vegetable prep or tea and coffee making.

- Talking of which... if you have guests sleeping over, it may be worth getting a small kettle and drinks supplies in their room. Spending 24/7 with someone is tiring, and a chance to grab a few minutes peace away from you may be the hygge they need to keep their patience.

- A teenager's bedroom can make a chill-out space with cushions and beanbags. Most teenagers seem to have a TV in the room, which can save cross-generational arguments about favourite programmes, or to add extra fun use a projector and a sheet to turn the room into a home cinema. Take the games console up there and see who spends the most time there (top bet: the fathers). If you have a strict no food in the bedroom policy, it might be worth relaxing it just for the holiday period, so that party snacks etc can be enjoyed with no problem. Try and clear it of all rubbish, bottles etc at least once a day.

- Do you need to invite everybody over every year? I know the idea of a Big Family Christmas is deeply ingrained in our psyche, but is it worth having two sides that hate each other both visit at the same time and risk the inevitable argument? By including all of December and January up to Epiphany as part of your Christmas celebration, you can spread out the guests and separate the potential troublemakers.

- Let go of the Advert-Perfect image and just accept your family for who and what they are. If you, like me, come from a family of introverts, then accept they are never going to play charades or put on an impromptu concert for enjoyment on Christmas Afternoon. You will, however, get them to play a game together, or watch a film.

Entertaining the extended family and surviving it with grace and humour has to be about accepting them for what they are and releasing any expectations. If you get through the time without a major bust up or anybody storming off in a huff, then you've done well.

Presents: It is Better to Give than to Receive

Extended families can cost a fortune in presents. There's the time element as well as the monetary value to consider. And what if they don't like the gift you've chosen? What if you give a present to one sister that the other sister likes better? What if you fail to put in a gift receipt and then the item is on sale after Christmas and they think that was all you spent on them? What if you give a present they can't afford to return an equal value to? What if... what if... what if...

What if you didn't bother with presents?

Christmas was never about the gifts in the first place. In Victorian times if gifts were exchanged at all, they were small necessities, like some tobacco, a pen-wiper, a small needle case or pipe stand. They were usually left unwrapped and placed carefully on the Christmas Tree once it had been introduced by Victoria and Albert. It wasn't until the 1930s and onwards that presents became a big thing. And not until the rampant commercialisation of the 70s and 80s that BIG became a good description of the piles under the tree.

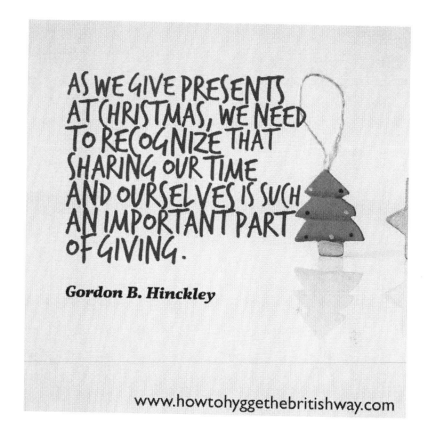

AS WE GIVE PRESENTS AT CHRISTMAS, WE NEED TO RECOGNIZE THAT SHARING OUR TIME AND OURSELVES IS SUCH AN IMPORTANT PART OF GIVING.

Gordon B. Hinckley

www.howtohyggethebritishway.com

Am I the only one who thinks it's gone mad? Am I the only one who reads the Sunday supplements with their endless suggestions of presents and thinks... really? A personalised nose clipper? A gold encrusted anything? Am I the only one who reckons that nothing would be a better gift?

In my childhood, true, I loved a pile of presents, but I didn't want the expensive stuff. I loved something to read, stuff to craft with, bits to wear and little things to play with. Books, especially, kept me good and quiet. And as I got older I needed less and less. I don't want my extended family to buy me anything this year. I don't even want a present off any friends. What I seek more and more as I grow older is time: time spent well with friends and relatives. Don't buy me socks, don't get me champagne. Bring a bottle of Prosecco and let's have a night in together.

So what's to be done? Well, there are a couple of choices to be made. Here are my top hints for making present exchanges between relatives and friends a little easier.

1. Give presents only to the youngest generations. For example, in our family this would mean no presents for the parents and siblings, but only for the nieces and nephews. After a certain age (like around 10) toys and presents lose their appeal, and money becomes a much more valued commodity, so Christmas present shopping becomes easier any way.

2. Give a family present instead of an individual gift to each member. A gift of popcorn, DVD, soft drink and sweets can give a family a fun night in over the Christmas break. Or source a reasonable priced board game. We like Exploding

Kittens or Settlers of Catan for families with older teenagers, but a few packs of Top Trumps could be fun, or a games compendium to while away an evening.

3. Give vouchers for something like the cinema, bowling or theatre trip. Sometimes the voucher acts as a reminder to the family to spend time together. Gifting an experience not an item is a gift of a wonderful memory to keep forever.

4. Only give stuff you know will get used up, not kept forever. Give food, drink or craft materials for the family to use. And don't give fancy stuff that the recipient will be tempted to save for a Special Day. Every day is special. Either give them the spices etc to make an Indian meal along with a firm date for them to make you one, or give them every day basics, just upped a level, like sweet paprika from a Spanish deli, or a jar of olives from Carluccio's.

5. Don't give any. At all. Save the money and all spend it on a meal out or a night at the theatre. Stop giving birthday presents and have a weekend away as well! You may not save much money this way, but you will get the reward of time together and a break later in the year when you may need it.

Most people would admit that their house is full of too much stuff. Their children have too much stuff, they have too much stuff. They won't thank you for adding to the pile, or for giving them anything that only ends up in the charity shop or landfill after Christmas, so cutting back on presents makes sense.

I would caution against giving homemade presents here as well, unless you know that the object is a. something they want or need and b. going to be appreciated. Hours spent on a quilt that then gets thrown on the floor of the car boot seem like a waste of your time and effort.

Let's be naughty and save Santa the trip.

Gary Allan

www.howtohyggethebritishway.com

And, yes, I know that you gift that to them and what they do with it afterwards is up to them, but it would still be heart-breaking for you. If you have to go homemade, far better to go with the gift of time. Make some certificates offering babysitting, gardening or clutter clearing services and then don't complain when they get called in. There are a host of printable certificates available on the web. All you have to do is fill them in and print them off.

Find an Extended Family Traditional to Celebrate During Advent

In Denmark, the Sundays of Advent are celebrated with family and friends. They gather together to make and swap cookies, or to make ornaments together. I think this is a lovely idea, and I could imagine it working well with a group of children and parents.

Hold a Decoration Making Party

My daughter often used to have a Christmas party on the afternoon of the last day at school before Christmas when she was in primary school. They broke up at 1.30pm, and I used to have the rooms set out ready for an afternoon of crafting. With a light lunch, some mug painting, paper crafting and sometimes either baking or cookie decorating, the day made a very special start to their holidays.

Choose the craft carefully according to the ages that you have:

simple card shapes for cutting and pasting can be done with any age, but you could up the skill level by trying decoupage, where pre-cut shapes or boxes are decorated with layers of thin tissue paper and protected by a coat of clear varnish. And for really crafty families, try a skilled craft such as porcelain painting, pyrography or mosaic making.

Paper hearts are a traditional Danish decoration, but I have also seen them made in material. Felt is a wonderful fabric, since it won't fray and comes in a range of colours. And using natural items to craft with is very hygge. Pinecones with a felt hat and cotton wool beard make cute nisse or gnomes, traditionally used as decorations in Scandinavian houses at Christmas time!

Pinterest is full of good ideas for Christmas crafts, but if you're inviting a group of children and their adults, why not ask each set to think of a craft idea to source and bring for everyone to do? That way the cost isn't entirely on one person, either.

Have a Timetable of Events that become a Yearly Ritual

Rituals in this context simply means a series of events that are done at the same time every year.

It would be lovely to have a set of extended family traditions, such as a pre-Christmas walk and pub meal one Sunday in Advent or a pre-Christmas cinema trip to see that year's blockbuster. If it always happened on the first or the third Sunday, it would be easy to plan for. Perhaps the local Church runs a Christingle or carol service that would work well. Go to the Church, sing your hearts out and then go to the local pub for a beer or cider together. It would take some of the pressure away from the time period around Christmas day if you knew that you had already had a Christmas event with friends or family and therefore weren't under pressure to see them again until the breathing space that is the New Year.

Organising time with neighbours can be tricky as well. Why not declare one Advent Sunday your Open House day? Drop a note through all your neighbours' doors and tell them you will be in from 2 until 6pm and they are quite welcome to come and enjoy a hot drink and mince pie. The chances are you'll get the people you know most at first, but if you make it a tradition and hold it again next year on the same Sunday, then other neighbours will come. It's a good idea to build community links, it makes for a happier world according to so many people. Making hot drinks and warming up shop-bought mince pies also makes catering easier, as well as meaning that you should have a chance to talk to your guests as the afternoon goes on.

This year our extended family (standing at 31 at the moment) are all going out to a Christmas meal the week before Christmas. We'll eat together, exchange whatever gifts we're giving this year and spend an evening in conversation and laughter, before heading off and celebrating Christmas Day in several smaller groups with just the immediate families. This is the inaugural year, but hopefully if it goes well it will become an annual event, with the number attending increasing and decreasing with the ebb and flow of family life.

Engage with friends in small groups rather than large parties

I am not a big party girl, so I would rather have a smaller group, but a better time. Asking just one family or group of friends around means you don't have to worry about big catering or expense, but can just plan an ordinary meal, only larger. And there's no need to go all Heston Blumenthal on the catering front, either. A large pot of chilli, a slow-roast piece of pork to make pulled pork baguettes or pizzas freshly delivered as the party starts work well. If you must cook to impress, concentrate on making a really gorgeous dessert and serving it with a good wine or beer.

Having a small group around leaves you time to concentrate on setting the atmosphere. I'm expecting your home is hyggely most of the time, with candles, throws and a comfortable, relaxed air. Christmas needs very little more, apart from a tree and some more candles and fairy lights. Can one ever have too many fairy lights and candles? I prefer the scentless candles rather than the commercial scents available, and then add the smell in the room either through a diffuser or by decorating using natural objects.

Small oranges and clementines made into pomanders, fir cones, branches of freshly-cut pine or eucalyptus can all add a layer of scent without the need for artificially scented candles.

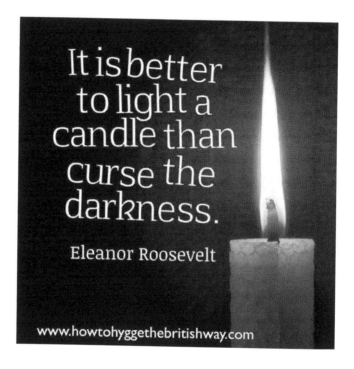

It is better to light a candle than curse the darkness.

Eleanor Roosevelt

www.howtohyggethebritishway.com

Light a candle held safely within a hurricane lamp in the porch window, or cheat with a flickering artificial light, to welcome your guests in. It's also really beautiful to see luminaries lighting up the garden path. Again, think carefully about fire safety. I have seen votive candles in large jars with a layer of pebbles or sand to secure them, or old tins with patterns pinched into the sides and suspended from posts or placed along the edge of the path to give a welcome flicker. And, of course, your home should have a wreath or evergreen bouquet on the front door.

Once in, encourage your guests to relax by offering them a comfy pair of socks, and use of a cozy blanket. And enjoy spending time together. Eating, watching a movie, playing board games or just sipping and talking. However you spend the time, it will be a great chance to build a relationship and enjoy the hygge.

Dealing with the Obligatory Visits That You Hate

In an ideal world, the people that we entertain would always be the ones we love, or like or feel connected to. In reality there will always be a need to entertain people who, for one reason or another, we don't get along with. They could be relatives, friends of friends, the partner of somebody we love or work colleagues to whom we owe an obligation.

Then it's hard to sit and bite our lip at the inflammatory remarks we hear, or not turn aside when parenting/handling partners/dealing with irritations is done in a way that we don't like or agree with.

I wish I could say all you have to do is….. and it would be solved.

Unfortunately I can't.

All you have the power to do is to try and keep the visit short enough to be bearable and polite, keep your own patience while going through the visit and then, when it's

Christmas entertaining should be about the people, always, and never about the stuff, whether that be the presents, the setting or the activity. Take all of that away and a truly hygge party will still be hygge. It will be you and a few people you really like and trust. It will be a place where you can all relax, enjoy each other and share a happy memory. May we all be so lucky in our lives!

Action!!!

- Plan out who and what you want to see over Christmas. Remember to space out people who may be a problem together.

- Talk to the extended family about how you want to celebrate Christmas this year. You may find you all feel the same and were all waiting for someone to raise the matter.

- Concentrate on time together, not things, and buy experiences, not gifts. Your house will thank you for it.

Christmas Hygge with your own House Elves

Other things may change us, but we start and end with the family.

Anthony Brandt

www.howtohyggethebritishway.com

Ultimately, Christmas (like life) is about getting the best out of your immediate surroundings. It's about building a life and a home that suits you and the people you share it with. That takes time, thought and often a willingness to compromise and adopt other opinions and traditions.

This chapter concentrates on your immediate household and the people (and animals) who live there with you. It should help you think through what you do and why you do it. It should give you some ideas to take away and put in place straight away, and other ideas that you may need to think through carefully. I don't expect you to blindly do everything I do... that's not the secret of hygge... but I hope you'll enjoy an insight into how Winter celebrations happen Chez Kneale and decide whether you can use any of my information in shaping your own happy, hygge Christmas.

Failing to Plan is Planning to Fail

I know this sounds sadly unhyggely, but the first thing I actually do when it seems certain that Christmas will happen on the 25th December again is begin to plan it. At some point in the midsummer I start lists of all sorts, to do with presents and things people said they wanted. Boys, especially, are usually very difficult to buy for. If I can see them look interested in anything during July or August, say, then writing it down to look at later makes shopping easier. This principle applies to extended family and friends as well. Have they expressed a preference? Write it down and you'll find it easier to buy for them when the time is right!

I keep my life in a notebook.

In September I take an evening off and get my Christmas notebook underway. For the past few years, my notebook has been in the form of a virtual notebook on Evernote. You can see in the picture below that I just make a checklist, then edit it. Yes, that is a list of the Christmas presents I wanted for myself as well as the ones I bought for others. At Christmas, one should always buy a gift for those you really love.

☐ Book on Kindle on Christmas Eve
☑ Dvd Mission Impossible 0
☑ Marzipan fruits

Me
☑ Red radio
☑ L'Occitane products
☑ The Chase board game
☑ Ally McBeal dvd boxset
☑ Spy Dvd

I also plan my Christmas budget then, with rough estimates on costs of items and the beginnings of a budget for each month, so that my shopping is spread out and balanced over four months rather than just one or two, or even worse just put on credit to be paid off at an unknown date.

I'd really recommend having a notebook or file dedicated just to Christmas. I keep important checklists in it for Christmas card lists, presents and the actions I need to do to have a smooth-running season. Again, for me these are Evernote checklists backed up by notebook checklists. The Evernote lists aren't dated, and all I have to do is check or uncheck the boxes when I'm planning Christmas. Keeping your lists as a word document to print out year by year is also highly recommended.

The List of my Lists would read something like:

- Still to get (I compile this one in early December)

- Christmas Shopping in October and November

- Early December Christmas Shop

- Christmas Eve Shop

- Christmas Clean Up

- Homemaking tasks Early December

- Housekeeping tasks in the Week Before Christmas

- Christmas Cooking/Baking plan for Christmas Eve and Christmas Day

- Christmas Movies to Watch

The human animal differs from the lesser primates in his passion for lists.

H. Allen Smith

www.howtohyggethebritishway.com

Because the practical side is so absolutely taken care of, it leaves you free to be creative with the house, or the days out or just to be free to hygge with the children knowing that the next thing you have to do is XYZ at such and such a time.

Let your fingers do most of the walking beforehand...

Dedicate an evening to trawling through the websites and finding the things they want. I love Amazon and Ebay for bargains and being able to get everything, but I love Etsy for the handmade gifts you can buy there, and I'm keen to buy items off independent shop websites if they have the particular things I need.

Either bookmark the page or save the link to an Evernote or Word document. They keep the hyperlinks intact as well, so when it's time to buy, it's a simple matter of clicking through.

But make any walking you do a pleasant experience.

When you know you absolutely must go shopping, make the experience a pleasant one. Set aside a couple of weekends, split whatever real shopping you need to do into two or three shorter lists and take a willing volunteer with you. I always try to take my daughter. We make a day of it, or at the least an evening, with a lot of window shopping, a stop for coffee, and afternoon tea or lunch depending on the time of day, some clothes browsing for personal use and the only real shopping done together and queueing together, so that the long queues become a chance to chat and catch up on the week's gossip.

Your notebook is also the place to keep your December timetable. Timetable is a posh word for a page with squares or a table marked out with all the dates from mid-November to 6th January. Mark down everything you are doing during the season, including any visits booked, events, school dates, church dates, and even the meals planned.

Decorations make a Christmas House

I know that Christmas isn't Christmas without presents, according to Jo March in **Little Women**, but I think it wouldn't feel very Christmassy without decorations even more so. Decorations in the house are the outward and visible sign of an inward and very excited child, which basically is what I am at Christmas.

Decorating the house is a real matter of personal choice. My beautifully festive corner will be someone else's over-done tacky grotto. Never judge, just accept that different folks have different strokes and that's all there is to it. That said, there are basic words of advice that can make your home cosy and hyggely without breaking either the bank or your back.

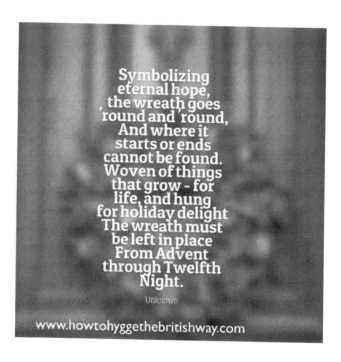

Symbolizing
eternal hope,
, the wreath goes
round and round,
And where it
starts or ends
cannot be found.
Woven of things
that grow - for
life, and hung
for holiday delight
The wreath must
be left in place
From Advent
through Twelfth
Night.

Unknown

www.howtohyggethebritishway.com

Start from the Outside and Work Your Way In.

I start the decorating of my house with the door wreath. On the first day of December it gets ceremonially carried out and hung on the same nail as last year and the year before. Putting it up on the first was a way of telling the children that Christmas was getting closer without having to go the whole hog and decorate the house.

The wreath you choose is a matter of personal taste. Evergreen wreaths are lovely, but can be expensive unless you make it yourself and have a good source of greenery. They will also need regular watering, so they do take up extra time. In return you get a beautiful link with the ancient traditions of the past, and a fantastic hint of seasonal scent as you pass in.

Fake wreaths may not give you the smell, but will yield better value for money. I had a fake evergreen wreath that I just added to with a bauble here or a jingle bell there. It was good enough for the purpose, which is to announce to the world that it's December and this house will be celebrating. Last year I found a beautiful white twiggy one that suited my style, so I've swapped to that one.

Now is also a good time to check that the rest of the entrance has that Estate Agent favourite, kerb appeal. A quick brush, a wipe down of door, steps and windows and the house looks and feels better. If you like outside lights, plan when you'll put them up and whether you need more. I'm a minimalist babe, so I usually just string a set of fairylights just around the door, rather than go in for big outdoor installations.

A pair of conifers on either side of the door can be decorated using tinsel or lights, or why not fill up a set of lanterns with cheap baubles in a variety of coordinating colours. This can be very effective and needn't be expensive if you buy the baubles in the post-Christmas sale. Pinterest (how I love that site!) has brilliant ideas for Christmas porch decorating.

And the power of external candles should never be dismissed. I wrote about some ideas for using candles outside in the chapter on Christmas Hygge with your Extended Family and Friends.

Bring a Little Christmas Cheer into Every Room

Well, mostly. You don't really want to overdo everything, so that taking the decorations down has to be spread out over a whole week, but having a small thing in every room that hints at the season is a lovely touch. It also means that you can introduce small things little by little and spread the decorating out to make it more enjoyable rather than another chore to add to the list.

Small touches like getting out Christmas tea towels in the kitchen, changing hand wash scent in the bathroom and hanging a small decoration from the door handles don't cost a lot, but give a festive feel to the whole house.

I like using the house décor that is already there and just adding a little bit to it. I might add some evergreen leaves to my rocks and pinecones, or place a handmade pinecone nisse on the bookshelves, but just a little thing can give the room a hint of Christmas.

I also like using products that add the scent of Christmas. I'm not a big fan of scented candles to burn, but I do leave my favourite Christmas candles open to let their scent gently waft around the rooms. I love Lily-Flame[30] candles, they have a great Christmas range, and new company Sandwick Bay[31] have a beautiful range of scents available.

And remember all those Christmas magazines that have the perfect Christmas image in? Well, we might not let their perfection rule our lives, but having a few on the coffee table or in the downstairs cloakroom or bathroom can be a way of getting Christmas imagery into even the smallest space.

---

[30] https://www.lily-flame.co.uk/

[31] http://sandwickbaycandles.com/

I try to keep my decorating to a theme or colour scheme. If you stick to one colour palette you can buy decorations 20 years apart and they still go well together.

I love red, so a lot of my decorations are red, or red and white. They look brilliant against a green tree, but very effective against a white tree as well. Red and white are, of course, the colours preferred by the Danes in their Christmas celebration. It goes very well with their flag, and they do tend to use the flag in their Christmas decorating. In fact, using the flag as a tree garland is popular all over the Scandinavian region.

The Christmas Tree is a Symbol of Love

Oh my! I found the quote below in an online search for Christmas Tree quotes, but doesn't it seem apt for anybody who decorates their tree with love and attention?

And when you think about it, isn't a symbol of love not money what our whole Christmas should be? There is no use having the biggest, the best, the most expensive tree/lights/decorations/turkey on the block, if you have nobody you love to share it with.

The first real decision for you, then, is real or fake? Real trees are lovely, smell divine and give a good old-fashioned or modern minimalist (depending on size and type of tree) feel to the home. On the negative side, they need watering often, present a fire hazard, cost a fortune every year and, if you buy a cut one rather than a potted one, are basically one-use only.

Decorating a tree can take some time, so make an occasion of it. Stick on a favourite movie or a Christmas CD, and begin to layer the tree up. You can get advice on how to dress a tree from websites like Home and Garden, but I'm willing to bet that, apart from the lights which should be balanced properly, everything else is more a matter of piling it on.

Have a traditional drink or treat that you always eat during the Tree Ceremony, like popcorn or ginger biscuits, and use it as a chance to reminisce about past Christmases. We have named and dated decorations, so remembering years past is made easier, since we know that the pink angel was bought in a year when Sarah was in to pink (she is no longer) and the felt pockets came from Newcastle, when Peter and I were on a rare weekend away.

Finally, make a fuss about turning the lights on. Stand back, admire your handiwork and enjoy the warm glow of Christmas.

Our tree lights are the second thing we turn on in the evening after a day at work, and it is beautifully hyggely to sit in a room lit only by candles and the lights on the tree.

Create the ambience you want in the House

The feeling of Christmas in your hygge house isn't hard to achieve, it just takes a little thought. Hygge is all about the little things, and using all five senses to enjoy the situation, so when you are planning or creating your Christmas in your home, think about that.

Keep lighting low; use fairy lights and candles everywhere that you can safely. Never leave lit candles alone for extended periods, and place mats below to protect surfaces.

Strings of fairy lights can be strung along mantelpieces or bookshelves to give soft lighting that you can leave alone with a clear conscience. I love the soft white tones, rather than blue or brilliant white. And a battery-operated string inside a mason jar or vase of pinecones is an effective decoration as well.

Add scent to your rooms using essential oils. A few drops pf pine balsam, orange, frankincense and cinnamon mixed with half a cup of vodka and half a cup of distilled water makes a lovely room spray free from any additives. I spray mine around liberally in the morning, as I arrive home and before guests arrive.

Bowls of oranges also add a gentle fragrance that increases if someone actually eats them. Food generally is fun to use as decoration at Christmas. Bowls of fruit, crystal bon-bon pots with sweets in, a pretty tin of **pebbernodder** left to pick at on the table. Of course, no Christmas food decoration is complete without a bowl of nuts and a nutcracker left out ready to crack them. Christmas is the season of excess and having piles of pretty food around is a way of showing that. Nigella Lawson once recommended using bunches of grapes, chocolate coins and clementines bought from the greengrocers with leaves still attached as party decorations and I love that idea. Decorations and dessert in one go.

If you are one of the lucky homes with a real fire, the chances are that you love to use it at Christmas. With the scent, sight and sound of a real fire meaning warmth and security, it comes very high on most people's hygge want-list. You can boost the hygge factor by using orange and lemon peel as kindling to start your blaze. It should give off a beautiful scent for a while as well as heat. Other ideas for adding scent include burning pine cones, using oils to fragrance your logs and putting herbs on the fire as it burns[32].

My home has a fireplace, but only a gas fire. I tend not to use it, since the central heating works well, but I like to light it up now and again with a string of fairy lights or to build a small fire in front of it using pillar candles or nightlights.

If you have neither fireplace nor real fire or want the effect without real flames, cheat and use a fireplace video. YouTube have several, including a 10-hour one with crackling logs. (I do know that several teachers have used this in their classrooms to get cosy at the end of a day: storytime by firelight sounds so good to me!)

With soft Christmas pillows and throws in your Christmas shades (mine are red, naturally) and a playlist of music that suits your style, creating the feel of a hyggely Christmas will be easy. Just add friends, a smile and some food.

---

[32] https://household-tips.thefuntimesguide.com/fire_fragrance/

Your Christmas Traditions will become Traditional, so choose them well

Traditions make Christmas for most people. Doing the same things year after year, eating the same food, singing the same songs. Traditions bind us together. For some, they are a necessary comfort. It is as it always was, as it always will be. For others, they can be a straitjacket, binding you to doing a thing 'just because'.

Traditions are hyggely because they provide a sense of security, but that doesn't mean you are eternally tied to them, nor that you must always do what has been done before. Sometimes a change is needed, and you shouldn't be scared to make that change.

It would, however, seem silly to throw everything out. Look at your traditions with a clear head. Look at them in the context of who you are and what your circumstances are at the moment. Then think through them, and decide which you want, which you need and which ones you need to change. Total change for change's sake every year would be discombobulating, so don't feel that you have to change too much.

Food, for example, is an area full of tradition that varies from country to country. In the UK the full turkey dinner on Christmas Day is expected. In France, the main Christmas celebration is on Christmas Eve and can involve up to 13 desserts in some regions!

My tradition is a large turkey dinner served at about 4pm on

Christmas Day. We find that cuts out any need for lunch or a tea afterwards, and leads very nicely into an evening of Doctor Who, Strictly and other TV favourites. I've moved the timings in the past to suit the circumstances. When we regularly had elderly relatives, an earlier lunch was better; one day I am anticipating a Christmas meal served in the late evening, with champagne. It may never happen, but I won't be too disconcerted if the tradition has to change. It's not one of my absolutes.

Make a chore into a part of the celebration.

Making rituals out of chores can be a good tradition: try present wrapping to a favourite film or CD of music with glögg or hot chocolate. Christmas cards needn't all be in your handwriting. Offer a takeaway or box of chocolates as an inducement to help. I think it's very easy at Christmas to have someone who becomes Chief House Elf (usually the mother) who has a vision of the Perfect Christmas and the Perfect Christmas House. That's seeking for perfection, and so uhygge. Release the ambitions, accept the imperfections and delegate with a free hand and easy heart.

Getting those who share your house to share the work is a good idea. It means that the Chief House Elf won't reach Christmas Day too shattered to enjoy it.

I like to write a list (no surprise there) of all the jobs I have to do before Christmas and post it somewhere prominent with a pen next to it. It includes all the baking, cleaning, washing, ironing, wrapping, card writing etc. I still end up doing the lion's share, but some of the easier but still time-consuming chores get taken off me. The bathroom will be cleaned; badly, but still cleaned. The cupcakes will be made and iced, dining room tidied, table set and I will still have the stollen to make and turkey to cook.

Organise Christmas Day to suit your family.

Hold a discussion with the family to decide when and how you want your presents to be opened. Until recently, we had three young children desperate to open their toys, so a general free-for-all on Christmas morning was the only answer. We tried to delay it with stockings on the bed, but we would still be up and ready to rip open the parcels by 8am at the latest.

Our eldest two are teenage boys, and the presents don't hold the same appeal, so last year we changed the tradition. Sarah and I got up early, to enjoy Buck's Fizz and some edible treats together as we unwrapped some little beauty treats and watched a girlie movie, until 9.30 when we had to wake the rest of the household and start the stockings on the bed. We opened our 'proper' presents bit by bit over the next couple of hours. As Chief Cook and Christmas Fairy, it's not unusual for me to save my presents for Boxing Day. I'm just too busy to appreciate them properly on Christmas Day. Perhaps my own Mini Second Christmas would be a good tradition to start this year?

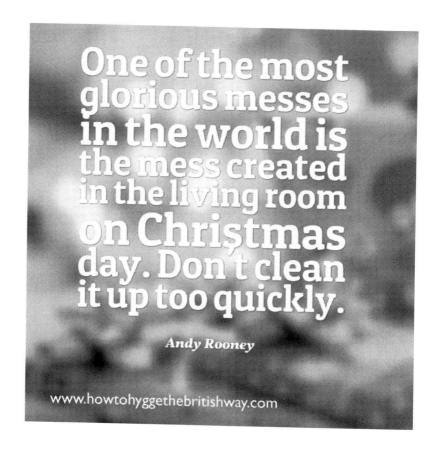

One of the most glorious messes in the world is the mess created in the living room on Christmas day. Don't clean it up too quickly.

Andy Rooney

www.howtohyggethebritishway.com

Start your own family traditions or keep up old ones: perhaps you want a family party on the third Sunday in Advent, or to declare one date in December your traditional day to see a film with your husband. As I wrote in the chapter on Hygge with the Extended Family, set it up and do it. Then repeat. Now you have a tradition.

Advent Traditions

I love Advent. That time of getting ready and anticipation means a lot to me. Getting the decorations out, buying the treats and food that summon up the scent of Christmas, seeing the house gradually change into a winter wonderland has always made my heart sing.

And I love celebrating advent as a family. I find that marking off the days until Christmas Day still makes my rather tall teenagers smile.

We have quite simple advent traditions. The first sign of advent is that we get the advent wreath out. I bought an iron base twenty years ago from a Cathedral shop, and each year deciding whether we have four red candles and a white central candle, or three purple and one pink candle with a white central candle, leads to much discussion about traditional colours, Church stories and finally an agreement that xxx will be the colour this year. We light the candles every night at dinner time, starting with the first Sunday of Advent and adding one more each Sunday until we have all five lit on the side table for Christmas Day breakfast. You can find explanations for what each candle signifies online.

We have one central advent calendar with red felt sacks hanging down. Three small chocolate bars just fit inside. I love having a little chocolate in an advent calendar, but I just objected to the cheap, disposable ones since the chocolate didn't actually taste that nice.

Packing the calendar is one of those chores that happily get taken off me. I usually buy a couple of big tubs of mini chocolate bars, and then Sarah sorts them out into the ones she likes and the ones she doesn't. That way, she tells me, she gets a chocolate she loves every day.

And finally, we have an advent calendar crib scene. These live in one of the wood/card refillable calendars that shops often have, but the figures were bought from Spain. My parents bought me the original crib scene, and I collected enough figures to make a village when I was lucky enough to visit as well.

As Advent starts, the scene starts with flamenco dancers but as the month goes by they are joined by villagers, Barcelona players and the medics to attend the birth. It's a great way of talking about the Christmas Story with children.

Christmas Eve Traditions

Perhaps because of the magical feelings of anticipation, creating traditions on Christmas Eve comes naturally to most families. I'd argue if you live in a couple or alone, then you, too would benefit from traditions, although they will be your own and vastly different from those with children. The next chapter has a section on Christmas Eve traditions for self-care that would also suit couples or people who live alone.

For families with children, my top Christmas Eve traditions are:

- Keep the afternoon free for unexpected visitors or events. You can arrange an afternoon of baking and cookie decorating, which children adore.

- Wrap up new pyjamas for every child. These are the first presents of Christmas. Slip a new book into each one as well. In Iceland, people exchange books on Christmas Eve and then spend the rest of the evening reading them. The rush of new releases in the months before Christmas is called Jólabókaflóðið, meaning Christmas Book Flood. I can't think of a nicer way to start the celebrations.

- It's becoming more popular to have a Family Christmas Eve box, with a selection of things in such as chocolate treats, hot chocolate sachets, new socks, new pyjamas, a film to share as a family, a board game or a small toy to play with. The idea is to take the edge of Christmas Eve and spread out the opening. Boxes can cost as little or as much as you like, but I would feel awkward spending a lot on a box for use once a year. Use your ingenuity and a more individual, frugal version will be possible.

Its Christmas Eve! Its the one night of the year when we all act a little nicer, we smile a little easier, we cheer a little more. For a couple of hours out of the whole year, we are the people that we always hoped we would be.

Frank Cross in Scrooged

www.howtohyggethebritishway.com

- Have an early bathtime. Use Special Santa bubble bath, and then slip into the new pyjamas, which have spent bathtime on the radiators getting warm.

- Have the evening meal off a plate in front of the TV. Watch a family movie, eat pizza and salad and just relax. An easy meal makes a complete change from the smart, formal meal of Christmas Day.

- Turn on the computer and track Santa. Norad[33] have a dedicated page where you can track the Big Man across the World. You could make Bedtime dependent on where he is… I remember telling mine one year that when Santa hit Saudi Arabia, they had to go to bed and sleep or risk getting nothing. It worked as well.

- Sprinkle some glitter on the front path as a sign you're ready. Mix with oats and seeds to make special Reindeer food.

- Read together. For the past 10 years I have snuggled up next to Sarah and read The Story of Holly and Ivy, a charming book about a girl, a doll, Christmas and wishing. Makes me cry. Last year I muttered something about "You won't want it now you're 14.". Turns out having a story read to you by your Mum is just what a girl on the cusp of adulthood wanted. Will we do it again this year? I don't know: I'll wait and see.

- Get them to bed at a reasonable time, even if you have to sit outside the door for a little to keep them quiet. You don't want completely wired children on Christmas Day. You should keep to whatever their usual bedtime is, as much as possible, then they stand a chance of a decent night's sleep

---

[33] http://www.noradsanta.org/

before tomorrow.

- Get everything you need to do completed before you get to sit down. The chances are you'll have to wait up for Santa anyway, so you will get a time to yourself.

- Finally, enjoy an adult treat before you crawl to bed. Pick your poison: bath, Baileys, new nightwear or bed with a beautiful person. Or all of them, and get a good night yourself.

Christmas Day Traditions.

Few things cause more stress in a family than when two different traditions meet over Christmas Day. When I was first married, my husband couldn't believe that at 25 I still wanted to wake up early on what, to him, seemed like a perfect opportunity to lie in bed.

I couldn't see how anyone could sleep when there were parcels with their name on under the tree, nor why he didn't see the box of Quality Street as a suitable breakfast offering. We had to talk through the issues as they arose, and I had to remember that, even though I love Christmas, some people don't get it and not everybody is ready to party at the same time.

Our Christmas Day traditions have changed slightly as the children came along and got older, but generally there are three big areas open to debate:

- When to open the presents

- What to eat for the dinner

- What activities are good for Christmas Day after the meal

Now is just the time to look back at the memories and wishes you collected in the introduction. Take some time to discuss it with the people who share your house, decide on these three biggies, and then just do it.

We have stockings on the end of the bed to start with. They've always been a convenient way to stretch out the morning by just another half an hour. It's also got harder to source them as the children get older. Sarah is easy: make up, books and sweets will make her happy anytime, but finding things small enough for teenage boy that won't just get a quick mumble and get thrust aside is getting increasingly harder as time goes by. A quick rampage around Hawkin's Bazaar[34] to collect a basket of plastic toys doesn't cut the mustard any more, it seems.

Then it's downstairs for a controlled present opening, breakfast with

---

[34] https://www.hawkin.com/

stollen and cake, before a quiet afternoon for most people and a mad afternoon of cooking for me to produce the Christmas Feast around 4pm.

Eating takes up a lot of time, and then it's time for me to collapse, knowing that my big work is done. TV, reading and present stroking, and an early night after a hard day and my Christmas Day is over for another year.

You will want to look at your own heart's desires and then temper them with reality. Families with children will have more restrictions placed on when and how to eat, simply because you will need to accommodate naptimes, not expect children to wait too long for food, and be ready to anticipate a tired, chocolate-fuelled meltdown at any point in the day.

Look at your current tradition for the day, and see how you can tweek it to suit your ambitions. As always, remember that people are only human and perfection will never happen. Discuss what other people want, and be adaptable enough to mix traditions if you can. If some people want to play games after dinner, while others want to sleep or read, can you make two areas? Or discuss with the more amenable party and arrange a compromise that is mutually acceptable? (Try bribing children: "if you stay at the table this afternoon for two hours, then you can disappear when Strictly and Eastenders is on with a bottle of cola and a bag of crisps" works very well)

And it's worth having a family game or two tucked up your sleeve. Ones that can be played without a lot of props or preparation are always useful to know[35].

Action!!!

- Think through the traditions of your family. Are you happy with them? Are there things you want to do or try? Discuss these with your immediate family and see what they feel.

- Write a skeleton plan for the month/days of Christmas. This isn't set in stone, but knowing that you are out the next two Sundays means you may look to stay at home the weekend after. Likewise, if you know Christmas Day is busy visiting, then plan a hygge day for Boxing Day to give everyone a chance to decompress.

- Use Pinterest or other websites as inspiration for further ideas. Be selective in what you finally do, though. Better to do a few things well, than try and do everything this year. Christmas will, after all, happen again next year!

---

[35] http://www.dinner-party-genie.com/games.html

Christmas Hygge with Yourself

Finding time to spend on yourself is difficult at any time of the year: and doubly or triply so at Christmas, when your time, organizational and diplomatic skills are heavily in use, and even the stresses of everyday life are magnified by expectation and the assumption that Christmas should be a happy season.

However, I'd argue that this is precisely the season to take time for yourself, and indulge in small acts of self-care that will help you to relax, enjoy a peaceful moment and then pick up the reins of the sleigh ride that is Christmas.

I don't want this chapter to be yet another thing on your to do list. The last thing you need is even more adding to that! What I'd like you to do is read the whole chapter, choose just a few that you know you can do and a couple more that you think you'd like to do, and then schedule them into your planning as firmly as, say, the visit to Santa or the Pantomime will be. Taking time out isn't selfish, it's a medicine. If having an hour off now to watch a movie saves you collapsing with a cold the day after Boxing Day, then that's time well spent. If getting out into the frosty air saves you having an argument with Aunt Mildred, then family peace is worth saying to those demanding attention, "No, I'm busy with an appointment until 3. Come back then."

Your Own Private Advent

Here are 13 ideas, all free or very low cost, some to be done alone, others with friends and family. They should all boost your mood or your health, helping to keep you on an even keel and better equipped to deal with the stresses that are life at Christmas time.

Advent Love 1: Advent is a part of the season.

So often we focus on the Big Day itself, especially if we're parents or hosting the whole shebang. That's a real pity, because anticipation really is a large part of the joy. Children have always marked off the days in one way or another, and recently adults have been able to buy advent calendars to suit their various interests: just a quick browse on Amazon showed calendars with beer, make-up, gin, candles.... Prices range from £10 to anything upwards of £200 for a proper golden jewellery advent calendar.

Collating your own calendar can be fun and need not be expensive. For the past few years I have used a white and red fabric calendar and filled the tiny pockets with a teabag, a square of chocolate or other sweet treat and an action or thought for the day. Yes, there are days when I'm trying to fit in three cups of tea to make up for the days I've missed, but if I can set out to have a 15-minute break at some point in the day to sip my tea and nibble the chocolate, then I know I at least have the chance of a pause in my life.

Why not start as soon as Christmas hits your awareness and collect teabags or coffee sachets, sweets, samples of toiletries, charity shop books, dvds or cds and wrap them up as an advent gift to yourself. It does come highly recommended.

Advent Love 2: Set up a Gratitude Jar.

This works like a gratitude journal, except it's on show. Find a suitable sized jar (between 1 litre and 2 litres works best), cut small squares of white or coloured paper and keep with a pen next to the jar. When good things happen, record them and keep them in the jar, until New Year's Eve or Day, when you can start the year off with a blast of happy positivity.

Advent Love 3: Start a Self-Care list

Write out a list of all the things that make you feel relaxed or happy e.g. having a bubble bath by candlelight, drinking tea from your favourite mug, reading a magazine. Include the simple acts of self-care that sometimes get overlooked at this time of year, like painting your nails, or chatting to an old friend. Keep it in your planner, or print it out for your kitchen wall and look at it when the spare 10 minutes turns up. Having the suggestions ready makes using those 10 minutes on self-care easier.

Advent Love 4: Find Your Favourite Hot Drink for Any Situation.

The power of a proper cuppa has long been known in Lancashire, where every entrant to the house is offered a brew. Tea is a perfect pick-me-up in most situations, but it's good to know there are other hots drinks available. Try a few, and see which ones suit your mood.

I love a proper hot chocolate, with whipped cream, marshmallows, chocolate dusting and a candy cane to stir. I may only have it once or twice a year, though, and usually when it's snowing or freezing cold.

I'm also partial to glögg, especially after a shopping expedition or if friends call round. You will find countless recipes for it on the internet. If alcohol is off limits, then a spiced apple drink can be beautiful. Simply heat apple juice with 3 star anise, 2 cloves and a crumbled cinnamon stick. Add a sliced lemon and clementine, then gently heat until hot but not boiling. Infusing for 10 minutes allows the flavours to mix more readily.

Advent Love 5: Give yourself permission to nest.

Have you ever let yourself stay in bed for as long as you wanted to? Usually we only use the power of our beds when we're ill, but giving yourself permission to stay in bed for an extra hour or more could be just the tonic you need. You're free to sleep, if you need to, but I love spending time in bed just reading, writing or listening to stories on Audible.

If I'm being truly decadent, I make sure I have a selection of comfy cushions, a cosy cardigan and easy access to a warm drink and/or snack. Toast truly isn't the best thing for bed picnics (too many crumbs) but making a warm bowl of porridge and taking it back with you, or eating cheese on toast with a side of tomato soup can be.

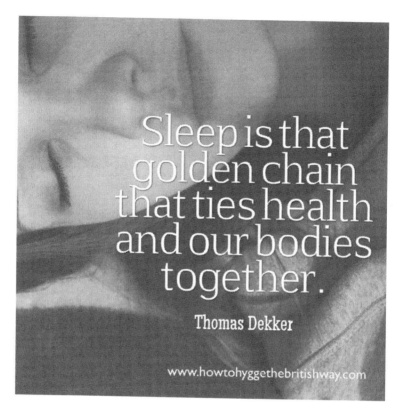

Sleep is that golden chain that ties health and our bodies together.

Thomas Dekker

www.howtohyggethebritishway.com

Of course, you can always choose to use your extra time in bed with a partner in whichever way you prefer.

Advent Love 6: Collect together your Hygge Clothes and Use Them.

When hygge hit it big in Winter 2016, the instafeeds were full of faux fur throws and cashmere socks and throws. I do apologise if you are a big cashmere sock fan but... really? Given the amount of looking after real wool anything needs, it would seem doubtful that anything really rich and luxurious could give you a hyggely feeling everyday. I'd be too worried about spills and stains.

Collect comfortable clothing that is easy wear and easy care. If you have them already, well done and Gold bless you! But if you need to get some, then check for washable, good texture and a good size. A bodycon dress will never be hyggely, nor will anything else too restrictive. That doesn't mean, of course, that you need to look scruffy. Chuck out anything too battered or worn. The aim is to be happily relaxed, while still looking decent enough to open the door to the Carol Singers when they arrive.

Advent Love 7: Treat Yourself Between Christmas And New Year.

In my house we have a tradition which we started when the children were very young and received loads of presents on Christmas Day. We held back a selection of gifts and gave them one a day for the week between Christmas and New Year. It helped to spread the fun and excitement, and meant that they were never over-faced by the choice.

I still do it now, and although the children do get less on Christmas Day, they get something good every day between. It could be a book, make-up, a DVD or a kit. It means they never hit the point of diminishing returns, where they have so much stuff they can't pay attention to anything. I always wanted to avoid the Brat Tantrum because the 15th present was something Useful and Not What They

Asked For.

I'd love to say treat yourself to a gift every day for a week, but that would soon mount up both in terms of money and stuff in your house. Instead, in the week between Christmas and New Year, give yourself the treat of indulging in time to waste. If you're a parent, grab nap time or a time when they are busy playing and just zone out. Grab your headphones and listen to a meditation app, such as Headspace, or a chapter of a book on Audible. Sit down, shut out the world and warn anybody who disturbs you that they will be In Serious Trouble.

Advent Love 8: Disconnect

It's very easy to spend a lot of free time on Social Media, especially if, like me, social media actually plays a big part in the job you do. In a normal week I will write 2 or 3 blogposts, share them, share the witty sayings I use to illustrate my books, create infographics and more besides for the Office Ninja job.

During December I actually post less than usual. I may do a fair bit of scrolling and liking, but I don't have the time to create the content. And, do you know what? I feel better for it. I give myself full permission to leave the phone upstairs, or in my bag, and not to bother with it unless I need IMDb during the Christmas movie.

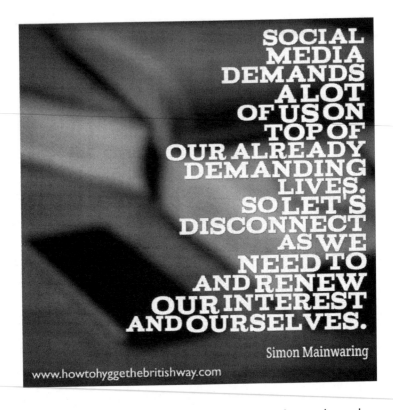

SOCIAL MEDIA DEMANDS A LOT OF US ON TOP OF OUR ALREADY DEMANDING LIVES. SO LET'S DISCONNECT AS WE NEED TO AND RENEW OUR INTEREST AND OURSELVES.

Simon Mainwaring

www.howtohyggethebritishway.com

It's also good to consciously disconnect: to take a day where you limit screen time seriously and concentrate on those things you say you're going to do, but never have the time for, like go for a walk, meet a friend for coffee, sew, knit, build the model of HMS Victory you've had since you were 14. Take a day off from the world: it will still be there when you step back on.

Advent Love 9: Read a book. Or two.

Have a list of books that you want to read in your planner, or buy a couple of them and keep them in a pile by your bed. Make yourself a promise that you will read one of them in a day sometime in December.

I read last thing at night, but it's not unheard of for me to find a book I enjoy and read it at every available (and unavailable) opportunity. Cooking, on the toilet, when travelling, in the evening. If you've found a good book, then nothing need stand in your way. If you're a parent, tell yourself you are setting a very good example and Teacher would be proud.

Advent Love 10: Meet up with a Mate.

Arrange a coffee in a local shop, get together for a Christmas Lights walk, just hang out for an hour at your house, watch a film at the cinema or, if your friend lives a long way away, book in a Skype call at a time that suits you both. Laughing with a friend is such a good stress reliever, and will do both of you the world of good.

If your conscience really starts bothering you, do something useful together, like bake or cook meals for the freezer, wrap presents together, or even clean each other's houses (only for really good friends!!) The point is to be with someone you enjoy spending time with.

Advent Love 11: Spend quality time with your partner.

Quality time was a popular phrase amongst the busy parents at the private school where I worked. "I don't get home until 8pm but we get half an hour quality time then" was usually given as a response to any implication that Johnny was tired, or playing up for attention.

In this case, Quality Time is a space when you and your partner get together to enjoy just being together. What you do with that time is up to you, heaven knows, it being a free world.

I do know it can be bliss to get out for a walk, go for coffee or watch a movie. It can be even nicer to get any children looked after by friends or relatives for the night, grab an easy meal and spend the night together. Either option is hyggely.

Turn off the phones, breathe deeply, relax and just enjoy time spent with somebody you love. It's good for both your sakes.

Advent Love 13: Create a hygge nook of your own.

Do you have a favourite chair or corner of the settee that is yours? Make it into an enticing Christmas Hygge Nook with some cushions, a throw folded over the back, a pile of books or magazines ready to read and a basket with some spiced tea sachets, a craft project, some hand cream and some letter writing paper. Use it as a place to unwind when you feel the need.

Having a scented candle nearby can also help you relax. Lavender, balsam, spiced scents and peppermint can all be relaxing. If you don't like scented candles, then a proper fabric handkerchief and a few drops of essential oil work as well.

Advent Love 13: Make a ritual of your Post-Christmas time

It's very easy to think of Christmas as just the days leading up to the 25th, but there are at least seven days afterwards that can be full of stress and worry. Make at least some of these days into your ritual year cleaning and planning session.

Planning is bringing the future into the present so that you can do something about it now.

Alan Lakein

www.howtohyggethebritishway.com

Grab your drink, your planner and your notebook and work through some short questions.

- What did you achieve last year? What helped you achieve

these?

- What did you not achieve last year? What were the reasons for this?

- What do you want to achieve this year? Think about your home, work, body and mind.

- What steps do you need to take?

Break down the steps into even smaller steps, and schedule the first ones in for the New Year. The journey of a thousand miles starts with a single step, and sometimes we need the push of a new season or new year to make that jump.

You can find further suggestions for self-care at Christmas on my blog, How to Hygge the British Way[36] or may I recommend Alison May's book, **The Christmas Countdown: Thirty Days to Festive Bliss,** which is packed full of ideas for making both your house and yourself feel pampered and ever so well cared for. I love her puttery treats, which have often inspired me in the past to keep a little Christmas magic just for me.

3636 https://howtohyggethebritishway.com/

Making Christmas Eve magical for you

I have written about Christmas Eve with a family in the chapter on House Elves. This is like an addendum to that... a little way that you can cherish yourself and help make Christmas Eve special for you.

First of all, have a special box just for you. Begin to assemble this in October or November. This will be your own Christmas Eve Self-Care Kit. I just use a small cardboard box, but I cover it in wrapping paper and keep it at the bottom of my wardrobe.

Tuck in small things that make you relax. You could slip in some bubble bath, a hand cream sample, a small box of chocolates or your favourite savoury treat, a small bottle of something fizzy, a book or a DVD of your favourite Christmas movie. Add a new pair of slouchy socks and perhaps a new pair of pyjamas and you're good to go.

Once the children are in bed, and the list of preparations for Christmas is complete, then open your box, use your presents to hygge yourself, enjoy a short period of relaxation and then slide into bed with a smile.

When my children were very little, my husband and I used to take it in turns to slip off to Midnight Service at the local church. It started at 11pm and lasted until just past midnight, when it was only polite on the parent left at home to forego the mulled wine and mince pie to return home for the last inevitable wrapping and present stacking.

The Midnight Service was always a quieter, more devotional service than most, so very often it was an hour of peace and reflection on a night packed with everything else. We now take the children with us, and have done ever since they stopped believing in Father Christmas as the provider of presents. It's the only time I ask them to attend Church now, and I ask them on the understanding that I know they profess not to believe, and attend as a gift to me rather than as an act of worship themselves. It's still a time of reflection for them, all be it accompanied by carols and bible readings.

Can The Day Itself Ever Be Relaxing?

If you're the cook, the answer is quite probably no. Although the meal is basically just a glorified Sunday Roast, because of the extra sides and the pressure to 'up your game' in front of any guests, then there will always be a degree of stress involved in Christmas Day.

Even as a guest of a friend or relative there will be tension involved. How much help can you give without it being too much or too little? Are you staying over? Do you get along with everybody there? You will need to be the mature person who finds a way to keep out of any family arguments, or find a way to diffuse them. I hate drinking too much alcohol, but I know for some families it's what they traditionally do on Christmas Day. Read the chapter on Hygge with Your Wider Circle of Family and Friends for more advice on coping with too many people and not enough space, and remember that you will always have the choice of how you react to events. Your attitude will establish your response, so cultivate a calm exterior, smile, and remind yourself that life is lovely now and will be again.

Build in your own pauses in the day. Escape to the bathroom and lock the door for 10 minutes, take a walk around the garden and breathe the air, accept that you are only responsible for your own attitude to life and that you probably won't please everybody all the time and, at the end, be very firm about the idea that after the meal and the many cups of tea are drunk, you are not in charge of the washing up.

Once your responsibilities are discharged, grab your drink, commandeer a seat that you know to be comfortable and settle down for an evening with the people you love. The clean-up will wait until tomorrow.

Self care isn't selfish, it's a necessary part of a healthy and happy Christmas. I hope my thoughts and ideas will help you to think through your celebrations and to endeavor to make them suit you as much as possible. Make the time about enjoying the little things of life, make time for people and appreciate the good things that life has to offer.

And when all else fails, you can always just enjoy the simple pleasure of spending time with your favourite child (mine being my darling daughter, Sarah, who helped me proof-read the book)

Action!!!

- Compile the list of treats you like best. Only by recognising and enjoying the things that make you happy, will you become happy.

- Start collecting small things for your Christmas box. You don't need to spend a fortune, save any free samples you get, or buy travel sizes in toiletries.

- If you'd prefer a surprise, ask a friend to compile a Christmas Box for you, while you create a box for her. You can set a price limit, and settle back to enjoy a surprise each day!

- Just do it. Take care of yourself. You know it makes sense.

A Word About Social Media and Christmas

Social media is here to stay. There is so much good to be found in Facebook, Twitter and Instagram in terms of communication and maintaining contact with those we love who live so far away. My personal Facebook feed is very often stuffed around this time of year with the pictures of cousins and friends who live too far away to visit, but who want to share the magical moments of the season with others.

There is also a darker side to social media, full of envy, feeling inadequate and the Fear of Missing Out when everybody else has such good stuff to post and you stick your little sausage roll on there.

I'm here to say banish the bad thoughts. You are perfect just the way you are, and your life is perfect as long as it suits you. Because as long as it suits you, who else does it need to suit?

In fact, the best advice for Social Media over Christmas is why bother? You'll be having too good a time to want to share, really. Put the phone down for Christmas Day except to use as a camera, don't check emails or updates, and live in the moment. You can always mark aside a half hour on Boxing Day to upload your photos.

Catch up on close friends and see what the celebrity gossip is, after a day off. Make it part of your self-care routine, but do it with the awareness that your life is your life, as perfect or as far from perfect as it may be, and no amount of looking at other people's feeds will change it.

Live in the present not for the present

www.howtohyggethebritishway.com

Christmas Resources: Books, Articles, Movies and More...

Top Christmas Reads

This is not a limitless list of Christmas books that I looked up and copied off Amazon. All of these books are owned by me and I have used them all in years past and present. Some of them are craft books that I peruse for inspiration, a couple are books that go into the whys and wherefores of celebration. I highly recommend them all, as a way to really examine your celebrations and keep them in line with your life values.

Unplug the Christmas Machine by Jo Robinson: This book has been reprinted 19 times, for the simple reason that when it comes to making your Christmas more value-centric, very few books compare to this one. I read it first over 15 years ago, and it had an impact on the way I celebrate.

A Chic and Simple Christmas: (Celebrate the holiday season with ease and grace) by Fiona Ferris is a short but sweet read on how to make your Christmas more you. Keeping Christmas authentic to you is hard in the face of cultural expectations. It deals with all the little irritations of Christmas and shows you how the author deals with them as well.

Scandi Christmas by Christiane Bellstedt Myers. This beautifully photographed book has 45 easy-to-make projects that will give your home a Scandi look for the holidays. With papercrafts, natural resources, fabric crafts and even a chapter on cinnamon and gingerbread, it covers most skill levels.

Handmade Scandinavian Christmas: Everything you need for a simple homemade Christmas by Hege Barnholt. With a variety of recipes and craft projects all with a strong Scandinavian theme, this book is about decorating your home using natural materials and with elegant simplicity.

The Christmas Countdown: Thirty Days to Festive Bliss by Alison May. Alison writes beautiful and sweet (in a good way) books that help you approach most of life with a spring in your step and a song in your heart. The Christmas Countdown is 30 days of puttery treats, lists, ideas and actions to make Christmas not easier, since nothing can do that, but prettier and more enjoyable. Ideas such as buying new slippers to celebrate the Feast of St Nicholas and using a rosemary bush in the kitchen instead of a tree. It's only available as a Kindle e-book, but Alison also blogs at Brocante Home.

Christmas Articles to Help You have a Hyggely Christmas

These are the articles I found and used as research during the writing of this book. Some I referenced in the text, most I found gave me something to think about.

https://www.theguardian.com/lifeandstyle/2016/dec/24/8-social-media-no-nos-christmas-day A useful article, with 8 social media no-nos to help you navigate the tricky waters of Christmas Over Sharing.

https://bemorewithless.com/a-guide-to-simple-holidays/ Courtney Carver is a minimalist hero for a reason. Here in one post she explains how to simplify the whole season and, even more importantly, why.

http://www.visitdenmark.com/copenhagen/attractions/top-christmas-hygge-experiences-copenhagen From the official Danish Tourist Board website: a list of 10 truly hygge things to do at Christmas time in Copenhagen. With the possible exception of visiting a Christmas Market, shopping isn't one of them. Spending time with family and friends and doing things together is.

http://www.huffingtonpost.co.uk/melanie-haynes/how-to-bring-danish-hygge-to-your-home_b_8344886.html Melanie Hayes, of the Delige Days blog, shares her simple list of what makes a hygge Christmas.

https://www.alsohome.com/blog/christmas/hygge-5-tips-hygge-christmas/ In Autumn 2016 the world was full of articles about how to create a hygge Christmas. This, by the founder of Also Home, is one of the prettiest and the most succinct.

https://hungrysquirrels.wordpress.com/2015/12/23/have-yourself-a-very-hygge-christmas/ I love this article for the stories she shares about her Grandfather Møller, whose nickname was Happy. She captures the links between Christmas and hygge in the last line of the post: "Christmas for me really sums up Hygge – family, dark nights, low lighting with candle light and fairy lights, cosy blankets, and the warming, comforting scent of the Christmas tree, and the smiles that the decorations bring. All these things encapsulate cosiness, security, familiarity, comfort, reassurance, fellowship, simpleness and living well."

https://www.sallyakins.com/hygge-christmas/ From a blogger I'd never met before, I found this article in a search for Have Yourself a Hygge Little Christmas. I think Sally catches the point of hygge (that it doesn't cost money and you have everything you need for it already) very well. Go get your duvet and let's hang.

http://www.livinghygge.co.uk/uncategorized/have-yourself-a-hygge-christmas/ From the curators of the original subscription hygge box, a simple list of nine useful points to bear in mind when hoping for a hygge Christmas. I love the advice to take loads of walks.

http://www.independent.co.uk/life-style/health-and-families/features/how-to-avoid-arguments-on-christmas-day-according-to-a-relationship-counselor-a6760226.html Avoid the booze and have a plan. Good advice from a Relate counsellor.

http://www.telegraph.co.uk/topics/christmas/6719458/Why-do-we-spend-so-much-of-Christmas-arguing.html Outlines the timetable of a usual family Christmas (in a beautifully humorous way!)

https://www.supersavvyme.co.uk/family-life/fun-activities/article/festive-family-survival-guide A sensible survival guide to the Big Family Christmas. It also has links to some free printables that are useful in your Christmas planning.

http://www.wow247.co.uk/2014/12/19/christmas-day-with-your-family-survival-guide/ Send this link to anybody aged between 20 and 30 and un-married. It's a survival guide from the point of view of the returning child. Love the point about the old room and the 'back up chairs'. They're yours "because you're a trooper. You're willing to take the burden so more high-maintenance family members can get the matching seats. It's not the chair you deserve, but it's the one you need right now. Because you can take it."

http://www.mirror.co.uk/news/uk-news/christmas-survival-guide-you-your-9445414 Another extended family survival guide. This one has good advice on handling moody teens: don't. Just get on with Christmas around them. The chances are whatever you do will be wrong, so let them join in or not as the mood takes them.

http://www.fyidenmark.com/christmas.html What do the Danes do to celebrate Christmas? This simple page has the major points explained.

https://tahnicullen.wordpress.com/2014/12/22/5-reasons-why-this-non-jew-celebrates-hanukkah-too/ A Christian explains the reasons why celebrating Hanukkah makes her feel closer to Jesus.

http://www.kveller.com/actually-you-cant-celebrate-hanukkah-and-christmas/ And a Jewish writer explains why you can't celebrate both.

http://brighterblessings.co.uk/articles/yule.htm Ways to celebrate Yule or Solstice with your family. Written from a pagan perspective, this article has simple ways to mark a day that can be quiet, home-based and very, very meaningful.

http://thesaltcollective.org/celebrating-winter-solstice-christian-family/ A Christian perspective on the Solstice, and why this family celebrates it together.

Christmas movies that embody hygge in one way or another

Again, these are the movies in my DVD collection that I turn to again and again to build my Christmas feeling. I've selected only the ones that spoke to me of family, love, hygge and Christmas together. I apologise because I will, of course, have missed off somebody's favourite. If I have, you can always contact me in a variety of ways and let me know.

The Holiday (2006): Luscious interiors set in a cosy cottage or mill house. I'm not a fan of the American house, but I love the American plot line. Also, I love the recognition of the fact that people make a place home rather than wealth or belongings. I was never more gutted than when I found out Rose Cottage was a set. If I ever lived alone, I'd have a house like that. Only probably with more colour.

Little Women (1994): Simplicity and authenticity are at the heart of Little Women in both the book and movie plot. The Susan Sarandon/Winona Ryder version (1994) tries to catch this. Enjoy the simple decorations, the small family gathering of loved souls, and the gifting of the Christmas meal to those even more in need. Charity is hygge? Yes, because we can relax better knowing that others are provided for.

The Muppets' Christmas Carol (1992). Just listen to the words. It's all the ways that we find love that feel like Christmas. Again, warm hearts open to spending time with loved ones and an active attempt to improve the lot of other people is hygge. We, the Family, love this movie so much that we will often sit down together in July and watch this just to get the warm fuzzies inside on a chilly summer's day.

The Bishop's Wife (1947). When David Niven gets made up into a bishop, life at Christmas is actually less perfect for his wife, who longs for the simple things they used to enjoy. This oldie has Carey Grant as the Angel who helps her rediscover the magic and persuades David Niven that perhaps, just perhaps, the greatest monument to God is not a fancy tomb or bigger Cathedral but the ability to take care of all God's people.

The Family Stone (2005): Okay, this is a weepie, but the family celebrate Christmas well... yet there's a secret this year that outsider Jennifer Anniston has broken in on. Will Christmas ever be the same?

Christmas With The Coopers (2015): Four generations of the

same family are gathering together for a Christmas Eve dinner, unaware that the parents are planning to get divorced. It's a full-on schmaltzy Christmas Drama, but I liked the quirky touches and life observations that were so like **Amelie**, the voice over, and the messages that are given at full volume that ALL YOU NEED IS IN FRONT OF YOU.

Christmas With The Kranks (2004): When it comes to it, Christmas is a time for the family and community. I love this tale of a married couple planning to escape Christmas while their daughter is away and dragged into the Whole Christmas Performance on the sudden news that she is coming home. They need everybody to help them create the perfect Christmas for her. When the chips are down, they find that family and friends are what matter, not where the ham is from.

Home Alone (1990): Another family feel-good movie. When Kevin is left Home Alone, he just gets on with it, even to putting up a tree and wrapping gifts. But although he wished his family away, he is soon wishing they were back with him. I love the house in this movie, it's just Christmassed to within an inch of its life! But even more so, I love the fact that the message is that family (love them or hate them) is what makes Christmas.

E lf (2003): The best way to spread Christmas Cheer is singing loud for all to hear. Seriously, this movie is so good it should be available on prescription. It's a great tale of not taking life seriously, making a family work and trusting each other.

The Polar Express (2004): A great use of music and character in this movie. Tom Hanks loved the book, so when his friend said he was making it using motion capture animation, Tom was there like a shot. He plays about 4 characters in the movie, including the Big Man himself. As a family, we were careful not to watch it when the kids were between the danger years of 8 to 12, but we all love it now and watch it at least once a year. The bell still rings in our house.

Rise of The Guardians (2012): Yes, officially this is an Easter movie (because that's when it's set) but can a movie with Alec Baldwin doing such a good St Nicholas and dealing with belief in the Guardians of childhood really be anything else but a Christmas Movie? And there's snow! I love the elves in this movie as well.

Love Actually (2003): I hesitated so much about putting this movie in here. It always makes me cry, without fail. So many of the storylines are actually set up not to succeed, and the music can have me red-eyed in an instant. But ultimately this is a movie about love, the power of love and the fact that life without love is not a good thing to have. And Billy Mack is priceless.

My Christmas Playlist

Having a good selection of music available over Christmas is an absolute necessity for me. I start playing my Christmas CDs on November 1st, and get a full 60-day immersion in the music of Christmas. Here, for your enjoyment, is a list in no particular order of some of the CDs that are in my Christmas case.

Kylie Christmas by Kylie Minogue: A brilliant album. I especially like the original songs, *I'm Gonna Be Warm This* **Winter** and **Every** *Day's Like Christmas.*

Christmas In The Heart by Bob Dylan: An eclectic mix of popular Christmas songs and traditional carols, all sung with a deep gravelly voice. It sounds weird, but it is good.

Harry For the Holidays, When My Heart Finds Christmas and What a Night by Harry Connick Jr: I have loved Harry Connick Jr since When Harry Met Sally, so his voice is really Christmassy to me.

Christmas by Michael Bublé: Another smooth-voiced crooner. I like classy music.

The Christmas Album by The Pasadena Roof Orchestra; This is like a time machine back to the 1930s. With cover versions of most favourite Christmas songs, the music has a really fun Jazz Age vibe.

A Christmas Cornucopia by Annie Lennox: There's something magical about Annie Lennox's voice, and in several of these songs she has an old-fashioned theme, with recorders and fiddles.

Sweet Bells, While Mortals Sleep, The Frost is All Over by Kate Rusby: Kate has a sweet voice, and a soft Yorkshire accent. She also sings carols that are local to Yorkshire (like While Shepherds Watched to the tune of Ilkley Moor Bar Tat) and there are some unusual, but really beautiful carols on here.

St **Nick's Got The Blues by Blue Blood:** I'm not sure what genre this fits into. It's mostly guitars and harmonicas. I think you'd call it country... or western... or blue grass. Whatevs. It's a fun album, quite foot-tapping, relaxing and unusual.

Afterword

The Post-Credit Marvel Movie scene

Still here?

I guess you're the people who go to Marvel movies and wait until the very last second of the credits in case there's a second or a third post-credit scene.

I'd like to make it worth your while having read the whole book. I'd love to offer a golden hare or a free ice cream for showing such patience. Sadly, I'm an independent publisher, so I can't yet.

I can offer you my thanks again for buying the book.

Christmas is a special time of year, and I hope this book helps you to celebrate yours with authenticity and happiness. Hygge happiness, born of safety, comfort and joy. Let me know if you found any part particularly useful, or whether you read the books and watched the movies. I'd love to know the ones you recommend as well. There's always a missed movie or an inspirational book that passes you by. You can share it with me on the Facebook page for my blog, How to Hygge the British Way, or by finding me on social media. I'm on Instagram, Twitter and Pinterest.

I'd love you to hashtag anything you share, with #happyhyggechristmas, so that I can find it and feel useful.

I hope you did find this book useful. I hope you have a merry, peaceful, meaningful and hyggely Christmas. Let me know if you've found anything useful in the book, and if you've really enjoyed it then please leave a review on Amazon or on Goodreads. Every star helps!

J o K n e a l e will return

in

52 Weeks of Happiness

but probably not until 2018.

Made in the USA
Lexington, KY
18 November 2017